IMPROVED INSTRUCTION

Dr. Madeline Hunter

TIP PUBLICATIONS
El Segundo, California

THEORY INTO PRACTICE PUBLICATIONS

Motivation Theory for Teachers
Reinforcement Theory for Teachers
Retention Theory for Teachers
Teach More—Faster!
Teach for Transfer

Additional Publications

Aide-ing in Education
Prescription For Improved Instruction
Improving Your Child's Behavior
Parent-Teacher Conferencing
Mastery Teaching

Copyright,© 1976, by Madeline Hunter
TIP Publications P.O. Box 514
El Segundo, California 90245

Sixteenth Printing, February, 1985
Seventeenth Printing, June, 1985
Eighteenth Printing, October, 1985
Nineteenth Printing, July, 1986

ISBN 0-935567-06-2

PRINTED IN THE UNITED STATES OF AMERICA

To Robert E. Cralle,
the Superintendent who taught me
the value of professional development
and that it could be accomplished
in well designed staff meetings,
this book is respectfully and
affectionately dedicated.

TABLE OF CONTENTS

INTRODUCTION

TO THE PRINCIPAL AND FACULTY CHAIRPERSON:

Of the many factors critical to students' successful achievement in school, one of the most important is the professional competence of teachers. This competence is based on what a teacher *does,* not what a teacher *is.* When teachers' plans are based on valid content and sound theory, then implemented with an artistry that incorporates fundamental principals of human learning, *students will learn.* If those principles of human learning are violated or neglected, learning will be impeded.

Information about how to increase the probability of successful learning is escalating at an encouraging rate, so much so, that it is difficult for a practicing teacher or administrator to "keep up." Even when new information is disseminated, it often appears in professional journals in a form which makes translation into classroom behavior difficult, if not impossible for the practitioner.

The *Instructor* recognized this problem and in 1973–74 commissioned the author to design a series of staff meetings. This book expands that original series of ten inservice staff meetings to bridge the gap between theory and classroom practice.

Obviously, sophisticated classroom implementation of complex teaching behaviors cannot be achieved in a one hour staff meeting, but professional knowledge can be acquired and subsequently refined through practice and follow-up activities. In this book, an initial blueprint or lesson plan for each meeting is presented with objectives for the meeting. Then, suggestions are given for classroom practice and additional reading to achieve the long range objectives during the weeks that follow. By reporting back to the faculty group at subsequent meetings, teachers will develop more advanced insights and classroom refinements. A great deal of professional growth occurs during staff interaction when members bring knowledge and experience (rather than folklore or "recipes") to the solution of common problems.

We have deliberately not included a long series of references as they soon become outdated and may even discourage teachers from seeking valuable information in current educational literature. After each meeting, however, teachers can be encouraged to read the references. It is suggested that several copies should be readily available in the local school and not require "location" effort by the teachers.

1

Critical to the improvement of instruction is the realization that "one shot" learning can easily be forgotten, so the time necessary to work through the content for each meeting should be scheduled with *only one subject* for focus, staff concentration and follow-up each month. After each meeting, a brief, written, anonymous evaluation by participants stating what was most helpful and what should be changed, gives important feedback for the design of subsequent meetings.

It is assumed that the principal will be the educational leader in these inservice staff meetings, although the responsibility of chairperson for each meeting may be rotated among participants. Teaming in group leadership can be a growth producing experience. Regardless of who is the chairperson, the principal must become knowledgeable in the professional skills being acquired so the implementation of each skill in classroom practice can be recognized, encouraged and rewarded by that principal. Having one's principal be aware of and commend the translation of professional knowledge into classroom practice is a powerful motivator, reinforcer and morale booster for teachers.

While it may be anxiety arousing, it also is encouraging and motivating to a teacher when the principal visits the classroom and sees the skill that was learned in staff meeting being used. Real respect for administrators will be generated when the principal translates the content of each inservice meeting *into his/her own practice* as he conducts staff meetings, relates to staff, works with discipline, or takes small groups of students and tries out the new ideas and techniques him/herself.

In this book, the content for meetings is presented in a logical sequence for scheduling during the school year. Each meeting, however, is an independent unit and is not dependent on the content of other meetings having been learned. Consequently, the order can be changed so the meetings with the greatest relevance are scheduled first.

Above all, the principal and faculty chairperson should know that these teaching techniques work just as successfully with adults as they do with students. These learning principles can be used in daily staff interaction at school and in working with parents. You'll be amazed at the improved staff relations and increased professionalism that will parallel the improved instruction and acceleration of students' learning in the classroom.

Madeline Hunter

GENERAL INSTRUCTIONS
FOR THE LEADER OF THE MEETING

The meeting plans suggested in this book are merely outlines of possibilities which should be tailored to meet the needs of a particular staff.

Staffs vary. Some teachers prefer to sit and listen until they have sufficient information before they feel comfortable enough to ask questions or discuss the material. Other teachers immediately begin raising questions and interacting vigorously with the leader and with each other. While the latter situation may be more reassuring to the leader, those staff members are not necessarily learning more nor will those participants translate learning into classroom behavior more quickly or more successfully.

The leader of each meeting should decide whether to expand or omit parts of each meeting for a particular staff. Some teachers like to check themselves with oral or written "tests," other teachers are uncomfortable with this procedure. Some teachers prefer the intimacy and opportunities of small group participation, others prefer a total staff format with the comfort of each member participating only when desired.

It will be helpful to keep the following generalizations in mind as the leader conducts the meeting:

1. The participants must have information *before* questions, discussion or small groups. Pooling ignorance only wastes time. Consequently, they must have read the material, *or* seen the film *or* heard a presentation. Usually the leader needs to "prime the pump" with examples.

2. The leader should avoid the "best" solution, always stressing the full range of alternatives: "That's one good possibility. If it doesn't work, what else might we try?" will stimulate seeking alternatives rather than trying to find the one best thing to do.

3. The leader should be prepared with examples that will encourage alternative solutions and which include many of the possibilities that are being learned in that meeting or have been learned in previous meetings. Flexibility of thinking that doesn't stop with one possibility, but generates several alternatives, should be stressed. With each meeting plan in this book, examples are given, but the best ones are those that teachers have experienced themselves in the classroom. Those have real authenticity.

3

4. At the first meeting, teachers will be getting acquainted with the idea of professional development, and learning some principles and strategies that they will be expected to use in the classroom. This is very different from the typical staff meeting, so the first meeting will not be as spontaneous and comfortable as the meetings that follow. Don't be discouraged if the first meeting seems a little "stiff."

5. Each staff has some enthusiastic members who tend to dwell on personal matters or raise unrelated questions. Leaders can develop ways of dealing with these so everyone's dignity is maintained and no one feels "put down," but the group is refocused on the content to be learned. Each leader has his/her own skill and style, but here are some suggestions:

"Mrs. _____ has made that point very vivid to us" (referring to her personal problem), "Now let's look back at the principle she has been illustrating." (Going back to the content of the meeting.)

"That's an interesting observation, let's look at our outline to see where it would fit."

"Many of us have had the experience Mr. _____ describes, now let's translate it into what might happen in the classroom."

"That is certainly a matter of concern. We'll jot it down and refer the question to the principal (PTA president, Superintendent), for (s)he has the authority and information to deal with it at a future time." (The issue may be school related but inappropriate for discussion at this particular meeting. Examples of such issues are teacher personalities, parent personalities, grading, textbooks, schedules, etc.)

6. The leader must constantly scan the group to make sure everyone has a chance to contribute. The timid teacher won't raise her hand very high or won't speak out unless (s)he is called upon. The leader must be especially alert to any sign or movement which indicates a nonparticipating member would like to make a contribution. Frequent sweeps of the leader's eyes around the group will act as radar. At first this can feel artificial when used with adults, but teachers constantly use it in the classroom. Soon it will become automatic and it is amazing how sensitive leaders can become to the feelings of each participant. In addition, each participant will realize the leader cares how (s)he feels and how (s)he is reacting.

7. The leader should take time at each meeting to suggest additional reading from the books listed at the end of every section and stress that this will be helpful in learning more rapidly how to incorporate the content into daily teaching.
8. A few minutes at the end of each meeting should be devoted to summarizing the content and restating the optional reading so teachers go home with the knowledge of "Where I can find out more" and the "glow of having learned."
9. The leader should plan to be available for a few minutes after each meeting to answer questions, chat with any teacher who desires it to clear up any confusion, and assist with any personal plans.

Meetings are not only learning opportunities for teaching more effectively, but opportunities for principal and staff members to grow in group leadership skills.

It is strongly recommended that several copies of this book be available so teachers may do advanced reading of the content to be discussed in the meeting. The books are also useful for review after the meeting as well as for subsequent rereading.

IMPROVING STUDENTS' BEHAVIOR

MEETING PLAN

Long Range Objective

Teachers will demonstrate proficiency in the use of reinforcement theory in all their teaching with evidence of enhanced self-concepts and improved student behavior.

Meeting Objectives

Teachers will state four generalizations from reinforcement theory and the behavioral results of each.

Teachers will cite classroom examples of use and abuse of each generalization.

Teachers will identify one behavior in the school, on which there will be a concentrated staff effort using reinforcement theory.

If appropriate, teachers will identify one individual's or a group behavior on which they will work in their classrooms, using the generalizations from reinforcement theory.

Preparation for Staff Meeting

Teachers should have the opportunity to read the article on Increasing Productive Behavior on page 11 or read *Reinforcement* listed on page 10. If this is not possible, the principal or a designated member of the group should begin the meeting with a presentation of the material or by showing a film listed on page 10, stopping to clarify and discuss each generalization as it is presented.

Presentation of the content at the beginning of the meeting will mean that a discussion of the generalizations of reinforcement theory and the application of those generalizations to a school program will extend into a second meeting. This interval is desirable, as it gives teachers time to "digest" what they have learned, try out those generalizations and translate them into a valid plan for action to increase learning achievement and improve behavior.

Discussion

The discussion should include:

1. Reinforcement occurs whenever people interact. It is as inherent in human interaction as breathing. Consequently, there is no choice as to whether or not teachers will use reinforcement theory. The only choice is whether it will be used consciously to promote a healthy self-concept with feelings of worth and competence, or whether reinforcement theory will be used in a haphazard way with happenstance results.

2. All knowledge about human learning is powerful. Like a drug it can be used for good or evil. A professional uses knowledge to promote human welfare, not to further his own interests. Consequently, reinforcement theory is validly used to increase learning and develop productive behavior. When reinforcers are used as bribes or to further only the teacher's interest, they are being used without professional integrity.

3. Each generalization in reinforcement is neither right nor wrong in itself, but must be used correctly if it is to promote behavior that is more productive for the learner.

4. Examples of use and abuse of each generalization should be identified. The discussion leader needs to be prepared to cite examples in a wide variety of academic content and behavioral areas which are relevant to the students and teachers of the local school. It is important to identify what it is that signals a teacher that the generalization is incorrectly applied so that platitudes (always be pleasant, be strict at the beginning, then you can relax) are not accepted but discriminators are identified which will act as signals to teachers for appropriate and inappropriate reinforcers. Teachers should be encouraged to work with examples from their own classroom to build reality and transfer into the discussion.

7

5. After listing the four generalizations on the chalkboard and talking about use and abuse of each, teachers should design a plan of action to improve an agreed upon, specified and pervasive behavior (improvement of the noon recess as described on page 23, respect for others, finishing work, coming in on time, etc.). Beware of taking on the most difficult problem of behavior in the school. The staff must first develop skills in the use of reinforcement theory through accomplishment of a more easily attainable behavior. After that, when teachers have developed the "muscle" of professional knowledge and skill they can tackle a more obstinate behavior.

6. At the end of the meeting, the plan of action should be summarized, and responsibility assigned to one person (either a group recorder or the leader of the meeting) to record the plan, so each teacher has a copy of the agreed upon behavior, the ways that behavior will be achieved and the responsibilities of each staff member for reinforcing that behavior. This step of written agreement is critical for it is easy for the final decisions and agreements to be lost in the discussion, or for the teachers to forget in the press of subsequent responsibilities.

7. A time needs to be set by the group for evaluation of the success of the plan so necessary modifications and adjustments can be made. It is important to stress that seldom is an initial plan perfect. Putting that plan into effect is the only way that necessary modifications can be identified and adjustments can be made.

Follow Up

Reinforcement theory cannot be mastered in a single meeting or even in a month but should be the subject of continuing focus.

Objective and, if possible, recorded observations of the success of the plan should be presented for discussion and decision at a future staff meeting. Placing blame or giving excuses for lack of complete success is a temptation that should be resisted. The important questions are "What do we do *now* that will increase the success of our plan?" "How will we know if these changes are working?" and "When will we schedule the next consideration of the success of our adjusted plan and make additional modifications that are needed?"

Encouragement and support should be given to teachers especially to those who are also applying reinforcement theory to the goal of increasing productive behaviors in the classroom. Eliminating unnecessary questions in the classroom, encouraging relevant questions, starting assignments promptly, students setting their own objectives and directing their own learning are a few examples of productive behaviors that can be encouraged and strengthened by the use of reinforcement theory. As teachers exchange experiences and discuss ways to utilize reinforcement theory that *they* have found productive, a great deal of professional growth will ocur.

The Principal's Responsibilities

The most important responsibility of the principal is to use reinforcement theory as (s)he works with others. Using the positive reinforcer of approval for teacher effort in an intelligent direction, rather than withholding praise until 100% sucess has been achieved will model the behavior that teachers are expected to demonstrate in their classrooms. A *sincere* complimentary note placed in the teacher's box is a powerful and well earned reinforcer for application, in the classroom or yard, of learning achieved in the staff meeting. ("You were doing a great job of positively reinforcing those children who were ready." "John's mother was delighted by the note you sent home." "Good for you for using a well chosen negative reinforcer when the positive approach wasn't working." "You were wise to ignore Ruth's attention getting behavior. That's great application of the principle of extinction.")

Lest this sound like "manipulation," know that the principal is a powerful model in the school and his/her labeling of what (s)he is doing is an effective teaching device. ("I want to positively reinforce your excellent classroom questioning techniques. They are really exciting as well as effective!")

The principal also is an important model of reinforcement techniques as (s)he works in collaboration with teachers on discipline problems by (1) cooperatively identifying the *one* behavior that is to be changed first, (2) making explicit the behavior that is to take the place of the undesirable one, (3) identifying positive reinforcers for the new behavior, (4) developing a strategy for accomplishing the behavioral change. Working with teachers on discipline problems is one of the most effective inservice techniques a principal can use to develop professional sophistication in the staff.

A concomitant responsibility of the principal is to make knowledge of the use of reinforcement theory available to the parent body. Some sessions on *Improving Your Child's Behavior* using the reference listed on this page should be scheduled for PTA meetings or workshops for interested parents. By developing parent skill in reinforcement theory, parents and teachers can collaborate on assisting a child to learn and grow toward more mature and responsible behavior.

Dividends

A school staff, with intelligent and artistic use of positive reinforcement, can create a truly humanistic climate within a school. Students will know they are respected, are valued and are learning. Parents will appreciate the enhanced self-concept of their children as well as increased achievement and improved behavior. Staff will experience the self-fulfilling yield from professional competence and the reward of a pleasant and successful classroom.

For additional information:

Books:
Hunter, Madeline. *Reinforcement Theory for Teachers*. TIP Publications, P.O. Box 514, El Segundo, California 90245.
Hunter, Madeline and Carlson, Paul V. *Improving Your Child's Behavior*. TIP Publications, P.O. Box 514, El Segundo, California 90245.

Films:
"Reinforcement." black and white. 30 minutes.

"Increasing Productive Behavior." color. 30 minutes.

"Motivation and Reinforcement in the Classroom." color. 30 minutes.

SPECIAL PURPOSE FILMS
26740 Latigo Shore Drive
Malibu, California 90265

INCREASING PRODUCTIVE BEHAVIOR *

Knowledge about and use of reinforcement theory contribute immeasurably to success in teaching, both in terms of a student's learning achievement and his/her behavior. It is important to realize that reinforcement is always occurring. It is an integral part of human interaction and helps each of us learn productive behaviors. When we get satisfaction or recognition from doing something, our behavior is reinforced and we are more apt to "do it again." For the same reason, we go back to a restaurant where we have had a fine meal.

Due to lack of knowledge of reinforcement theory and because it was first researched with animals (so was the Salk vaccine) some people have misinformation and believe it is a mechanistic or manipulative system. Nothing could be further from the truth. *Reinforcement theory is one of the most humanistic theories* for it accentuates the positive, building on a learner's strengths and ignoring as much as possible any undesirable aspects of his behavior. A teacher, aide or volunteer who uses reinforcement theory is constantly looking for productive behavior and strengthening it. As a result the classroom is a happier place for students.

The best reinforcers are those that build a feeling of worth thereby enhancing self-concept and making the student feel he is competent. ("You're doing a great job, you should feel proud of yourself." "You're learning that very quickly." "That's good thinking." "You're really in charge of yourself to be able to ignore that.")

Reinforcement theory also is humanistic because, through its use, it becomes possible for *all learners to grow, improve and experience success.* Reinforcement may not be *the* most important theory in teaching but it is *one* of the most important. Clearly it is also one of the most useful theories for it is used every day, every hour, in every classroom. Knowledge of reinforcement is equally useful outside of the classroom, for reinforcement occurs in our interactions with family, relatives, friends, professional associates, casual acquaintances, sales people, in short with every person with whom we come in contact.

Because reinforcement is always occurring, we need to understand how to use it so the results are productive for others as well as for us, rather than results being happenstance or even destructive.

---

*This is a brief summary of the content presented in *Reinforcement Theory for Teachers.* That book should be available as a reference, for examples, for extension of understanding and for application of these concepts.

There are four concepts we must learn to apply in our use of reinforcement theory; positive reinforcement, extinction, negative reinforcement, schedule of reinforcement.

Positive Reinforcement

A positive reinforcer is anything needed or desired by the learner.

When a behavior is *immediately* followed by a positive reinforcer, that behavior is strengthened and will occur more frequently. The immediacy of the reinforcer is important.

Most learners need or desire:

1. The approval of significant others (friends, parents, teachers). When that approval builds feelings of worth and competence such reinforcers contribute to a healthy self-concept.

   Examples:

   "You did a good job of thinking to be able to figure that out by yourself."

   "Your friends really respect you for how fair you are."

2. Opportunities to do the things the learner enjoys.

   Examples:

   "You've done all your work correctly for four days, today you may choose whether you wish to do it or do something else." (Free time for having done a good job is a reinforcer to all of us.)

   "You've demonstrated you know how to work independently, so you may choose what you'd like to do."

3. Special privileges.

   Examples:

   "You've worked so well, you may be excused early."

   "You've shown me you know how to do . . . so you may choose whether or not you wish to practice when we work on it again."

Remember to reinforce students' productive behaviors (finishing work, trying hard, being polite, paying attention). Often these behaviors

12

are taken for granted. When they are strengthened by positive reinforcement they become habitual.

Sometimes a person unintentionally strengthens an *unproductive* behavior by permitting that behavior to be followed by a positive reinforcer.

Examples:

A student whines to get his way and it works.

A student cheats on an exam and gets a good grade.

A student feigns illness and gets out of an unpleasant task.

A student uses rude or clowning behavior to get attention and he gets class or teacher attention.

Extinction

A behavior is extinguished (or weakened) when that behavior is followed by no reinforcement whatsoever.

Examples:

The class ignores a silly remark made by a student.

The teacher seems not to have heard a request when it is made in an inappropriate way.

A child ignores teasing.

The teacher must make every attempt not to have some one else reinforce the behavior (s)he is seeking to extinguish. If parents are reinforcing unproductive behavior (whining, tantrums, avoidance of responsibility) the teacher attempts to enlist the parents' aid in a joint effort to extinguish the behavior. If this is not possible (and in some cases it isn't) the teacher can extinguish the behavior at school but it will take longer. Students can learn that different behaviors work in different environments.

Extinction of productive behavior can occur if a teacher, aide or volunteer ignores all the students who are doing the right thing and focuses only on the student who is out of order.

Extinction is not used correctly when a teacher continues to ignore a non-productive behavior but it is being positively reinforced by others. (The teacher ignores a smart remark that is made to get attention and the class laughs. The teacher ignores bullying but the other students give in to it.) Extinction is also being used incorrectly when a student is allowed to continue to practice a behavior which is unsafe for him or harmful to others. In these cases the teacher needs to use negative reinforcers.

Negative Reinforcement

A negative reinforcer is something that is *not* needed or desired by the learner.

When a behavior is immediately followed by a negative reinforcer two things can happen.

1. A negative reinforcer is useful because the behavior that is immediately followed by a negative reinforcer is suppressed or "held back" (but not eliminated!). Suppressing undesirable behavior gives the teacher time to TEACH a new and more productive behavior and follow that behavior with a positive reinforcer so the new behavior is strengthened.

   Example:

   A student says rudely, "Gimme that." The teacher responds, "When you ask me in that way I want to say 'no.' Ask me in a way that I'll want to say 'yes.' " When the student asks in a more appropriate way the teacher responds, (if possible) "Of course you may use it." If permission is not possible, the teacher reinforces the politeness by "I certainly want to say 'yes' because of the way you asked, but it doesn't belong to me so this time I can't. You were really a good sport to be able to change the way you asked." (positive reinforcer is the approval of the teacher)

2. A negative reinforcer can also be dangerous because *any behavior that removes the negative reinforcer is strengthened.*

   Examples:

   If not telling the truth takes away undesirable consequences, not telling the truth is strengthened.

   If "getting a headache" excuses someone from cleanup, getting a headache is strengthened.

   If crying takes away undesirable consequences, crying is strengthened.

   If misbehaving gets a student sent out of a class he doesn't want

14

to be in, or one for which he wasn't prepared, misbehavior is strengthened.

Note that a negative reinforcer signals a student what he should *not* do but it gives no information as to what he *should* do. Any behavior that takes away the negative reinforcer is the behavior that is strengthened. That is why it is *essential* that the productive behavior *be deliberately taught* and reinforced. By doing this, better behavior is learned by design instead of undesirable behavior by happenstance.

Schedule of Reinforcement

A *regular* schedule of reinforcement, where the desirable behavior is reinforced every time it appears, results in fast learning.

Examples:

When a student is working on finishing his assignments, he should be positively reinforced every time he finishes one.

If a student is learning to make requests in a polite way, his requests should be granted every time it is possible. When it is not possible, he should receive approval or some other positive reinforcer for the way he asked.

But you don't have to keep this up forever, you soon change to an intermittent schedule.

An *intermittent* schedule of reinforcement, where behavior is reinforced one time and then not reinforced the next time, and the intervals between reinforcers become longer and longer, develops a very durable behavior that is long remembered.

Examples:

Once a student has learned to make requests in a polite way, the teacher will respond, "Not this time" or "It's Paul's turn." The next time he makes a request (s)he will say, "Of course, because you always remember to ask politely." The next few times (s)he will let fairness or the appropriateness of the request determine whether or not it is granted. The teacher must remember, however, to occasionally reinforce the way the request is made so politeness becomes habitual.

After a student has learned to finish his work, the teacher will change to an intermittent schedule of reinforcement. At times the work is simply accepted but occasionally his finishing is reinforced by, "You

15

really did that quickly" or "You always get your job done" or "I know I can depend on you to finish it so you don't need to have it checked unless you wish to."

It is essential that the teacher, aide or volunteer be consistent with reinforcers when a new behavior is being learned. If the old behavior is practiced on an intermittent schedule, and it works for the student, it becomes very resistant to change. It is equally important, once the new behavior is learned, that the teacher switch to an intermittent schedule so the new behavior becomes habitual and needs only an occasional reinforcer.

Because the teacher must reinforce new behaviors on a regular schedule, only a few new behaviors (often only one) should be the subject for special focus. Otherwise it is impossible to monitor behavior and maintain a regular schedule of reinforcement. As a result of being over ambitious, and attempting to work on too many behaviors at one time, the adult can feel swamped and be tempted to give up, for (s)he is faced with an impossible task.

It is wise to start with behaviors that are easier to change until the teacher develops skill with the conscious application of reinforcement theory. *Then* (s)he can take on more difficult behavioral and learning problems. (The medical intern doesn't begin with a heart transplant.) Most students respond well to the productive use of reinforcement theory and achieve better self-concepts as their learning accelerates and their behavior improves. A few students have such severe problems that we can't hope to "cure" them completely, but they too will show some improvement.

The productive use of reinforcement theory results in positive reinforcement for the teacher as desirable results in students' learning and behavior are more predictably achieved.

Here are some steps to follow in changing behavior. Remember, it's always easier to talk about something than to bring it off successfully, so don't become discouraged when the first results are less than perfect.

1. Identify the *one* behavior that is to be improved or strengthened.
2. If a behavior is to be changed, identify the behavior that is to take its place.
3. Determine a positive reinforcer.
4. Determine whether to try extinction or whether a negative reinforcer will be needed, if so, identify one to be used.

16

5. Design a plan for getting the desirable behavior, so you have something to reinforce.

6. Put the plan into effect and set a time for evaluation to determine what modifications of the plan are needed.

7. Evaluate and make needed modifications.

8. Continue with the revised plan.

An excellent practice activity for the staff that will yield schoolwide results is the selection of a common problem on which everyone will focus reinforcement effort as described on page 23.

Don't expect overnight miracles but do expect surprising increases in pleasant feeling tones in your classroom and playground, increased learning achievement and better behavior as a result of your systematic and artistic use of reinforcement theory.

For additional information:

Books:

Reinforcement Theory for Teachers. Madeline Hunter. 1967
   TIP Publications, P.O. Box 514, El Segundo, California 90245
Improving Your Child's Behavior. Madeline Hunter and Paul V. Carlson.
   Tip Publications, P.O. Box 514, El Segundo, Cal. 90245

Films:

Part III "Reinforcement Theory for Teachers." black and white. 30 minutes.

"Increasing Productive Behavior." color. 30 minutes.

"Motivation and Reinforcement in the Classroom." color. 30 minutes.

SPECIAL PURPOSE FILMS
   26740 Latigo Shore Drive
   Malibu, California 90265

USING REINFORCEMENT THEORY

A student isn't finishing his work. Here are some examples of teacher responses. In reality, however, they can be classified as positive or negative reinforcers *only by the subsequent behavior of the student.*

Positive Reinforcer   "What's the next thing you are going to do? That's just right, you're getting a good start."

Extinction   Ignoring that student, particularly if he is dawdling to get your attention and concern. Sometimes a general remark to the class or to another student concerning how much time is left, where to put finished papers, how to check when finished, is a way to refocus him on the work without giving him your direct attention.

Negative Reinforcer   "You will need to spend the first part of your free time in finishing your work."

Schedule Regular   "Let's put a plus on this card for every paper you finish—then we'll count them."

Intermittent   "At the end of the week we'll check on how you're doing."

DO'S AND DON'TS IN USING
REINFORCEMENT THEORY

1. Do let a child know, when he is really trying, that what he is doing is worthy of note.

   "You remembered to put your name on your paper so I'd know whose good work it was."

   "You had a good game without a single argument. You're really learning to be in charge of yourself."

2. Do let a child know he is making progress even though the work is not perfect.

   "That's getting better."

   "It's getting easier for you isn't it?"

   "That's coming."

   "Pretty soon you'll have it finished."

   "You're really trying hard."

3. When a child is learning something new or something that is hard for him, reinforce him for each part he does.

   "That's right, now what will you do?"

   "You did the first one right, now try the next one."

   "That's a good start, go ahead."

4. Do vary the words you use.

   "That's just right."

   "You're absolutely correct."

   "You got them all."

   "That's excellent work."

1. Don't be insincere or praise a child for things which are easy for him and take little or no effort on his part.

   "You did a good job of putting your name on the paper" (when he's been doing it for years).

2. Don't say something is really good when it isn't. Students usually know when something is not right and feel that praise for mediocre work is insincere.

   "That's great" (when he hasn't really tried).

   "You really know it" (when there are errors or halting responses).

3. Don't wait until he is completely finished with a *difficult* task before you give him encouragement.

   "I won't look at it until you're through."

   "Let me see it after it's all finished."

4. Don't use the same word for everything.

   "Perfect, perfect."

   "Very good, very good."

   "Right, right, right."

19

5. Do follow a negative reinforcer with a positive one as soon as possible.
"Look at this one again. Good. I knew you'd find your mistake."
"Not quite, look carefully and you'll get it."
"Why am I stopping you from doing that? You're right, I knew you'd know."

5. Don't leave a child with a negative reinforcer.
"That's wrong."
"You missed five."
"No, that's not right."

6. Do ignore if possible, behavior that is merely attention getting.
Ignoring the "blurter outer" and calling on someone who raised his hand (if that's what you asked the students to do).

6. Don't make a "federal case" out of every little incident.
"Now just what did you mean by that remark?"

7. Do remember to reinforce every time when new behavior is being learned.
"That's great Bill, you remember to wait until I call on you everytime.

7. Don't be inconsistent with your reinforcement when *new* behavior is being learned.
"You didn't raise your hand and we'll listen to you just this once, but next time we won't."

8. Do be specific when you reinforce a behavior.
"Good job, you're finished right on time."
"Good for you, you remembered to come the first time I called you."
"That's just right, you have finished every problem on the page."

8. Don't be so general that the reinforcer is ineffective, ignored or "tuned out."
"Good."
"Great."
"Fine."
"Good for you."

9. Do state the reinforcer as a recognition of achieving the expectation that was set.

"Good for you, you remembered to come in and go right to work."

"You finished all those problems in time, just as you said you would."

9. Don't promote "teacher pleasing" with a reinforcer that is a personal value judgment.

"I like the way you came in and got right to work this morning."

"You please me when you finish in time to go to recess."

10. Do determine what is a positive reinforcer for each child or group.

If they enjoy a game, "You've all been such good helpers getting the room cleaned up, take time for an extra inning in your baseball game."

If he wants teacher attention, say quietly to Jim as the group leaves for the play yard: "Jim, you were a good listener and remembered to raise your hand every time you had something to say."

"Jane, you listened so well during the story, you may choose someone to be your partner for leaders to the library."

10. Don't choose an inappropriate reinforcer for individuals or groups.

"Since you finished all the questions on this page, here's another set of questions to do."

"Look at how straight Jim is sitting, ready to listen and discuss the story" (when the last thing Jim wants is to be the center of attention).

STAFF COLLABORATION TO
ENCOURAGE IMPROVED BEHAVIOR

A stimulating and productive way to begin the school year is by concentrating staff effort on one student behavior that needs to improve throughout the school. Here are some possibilities:

1. Courtesy.

2. Behavior on the yard.

3. Behavior in the hallways.

4. Behavior in assemblies.

5. Being on time.

6. Keeping the school clean.

7. Caring for books and materials.

8. Fighting and arguing.

Two temptations will entice the staff. One will be, "Let's accomplish all of this." All these behaviors may need attention, but for concentrated (and effective) effort, the staff must start with only one. After that one has been accomplished and members have practice becoming focused and effective as a total staff, they are ready for the next accomplishment.

The other temptation is to say, "But these really aren't the most important aspects of education." While they may not be the most important when the problems listed above have been solved, teachers will have the time and energy to focus on more important attitudinal and academic learnings. Left as irritating and time-eroding interruptions, these problem behaviors drain off energy and affect dispositions.

A staff may also say, "We want to direct our energy to improving teaching so we produce learners who are in charge of themselves and are self-propelling in learning." This, too, can be accomplished if the staff begins by working on less complex behaviors in order to sharpen their teaching skills so that more complex learning behaviors not only become possible, but highly probable.

Here are some of the steps in professional decision-making that have high potential to achieve whatever student behavioral goal the staff desires:

Step I: Select one problem on which to focus effort.

If the staff is small, this can be done in a total staff discussion. Otherwise, the staff should divide into groups of 5-10 for an agreed-on number of minutes for initial screening of possible problems on which to focus staff effort; then report their recommendations to the total staff. The staff should select one problem from those student behaviors that have the highest incidence of staff concern. Don't get caught in the trap of not being able to agree on the most critical behavior. *Select one behavior and begin* even if an impasse has to be resolved by flipping a coin. Remember, the professional skills developed by the staff as they work on the first project will transfer and make achievement of subsequent projects easier.

Step II: Design a plan.

Having determined the student behavior on which the whole staff will focus effort, the next step is to design a strategy to achieve success. This will take the participation and effort of everyone.

To make the description of this step more meaningful, we will assume the staff has selected "improvement of noon yard behavior" so students will not come back in the classroom angry and frustrated from the problems they have experienced on the yard. The staff must begin by agreeing on a few basic behaviors such as the following:

A. *Students who play games will have the necessary skills and use one set of rules.* This implies diagnosing students during physical education and teaching, with focus on three areas:
   1. The playing skills essential to a productive and enjoyable game (throwing, catching, batting, kicking, etc.). Diagnosis will determine which skills emerge as needing additional emphasis. Perhaps one teacher could take a remedial group from several classrooms and really concentrate on (and measure!) improvement of skills. Proficient student athletes or older volunteers might be *trained* to be assistant coaches (the skill of helping another person learn also must be taught). Part of noon activity might be "skill clinics" conducted by the assistant coaches.
   2. The rules of the game, including situations where disputes are common. The staff must determine which games will be taught during physical education so they can be played at recess and noon and the agreed upon rules.
   3. Supervised practice of playing the games according to rules while the teacher is there to observe, teach to, or remediate

any part that is not going well. This must be done for each game—handball, dodgeball, soccer, four square, etc., as well as for correct use and replacement of equipment.

B. *Students not in games will be engaged in activities that are not problem-producing* (chasing) or interfering with the games in progress. The staff may need to designate a special area and develop enjoyable and constructive activities such as checkers and story-telling for nonactive students.

C. Arguments are inevitable in any group (witness your own staff as you try to agree on some of this). A strategy must be designed so students *learn what to do in order to settle disputes for themselves,* and what to do when, after trying that procedure, they are unable to settle a problem without outside help. Students must have practice in using that strategy to settle arguments during physical education.

Step III: Assign responsibility to staff members for supervising and reinforcing the practice of appropriate behavior at noon.

Getting the playground in order cannot be accomplished by pre- and post-noon admonitions. (You would not think of letting a learner make an error in math and then not give him/her help or correction until an hour later.) Students must practice the appropriate behavior and be reinforced for it *when* they are on the playground. Consequently, during the first two weeks of implementation of the plan developed by the staff, teachers will need to be on yard duty to TEACH appropriate behaviors at the time of the problem—not a half hour later. Aides and parents simply do not have the skills to do this. Once the playground is "in order," aides and volunteers will be able to maintain it for a period of time.

The staff must determine which teachers will be on the yard to reinforce good behavior, note problems, and keep the rest of the staff informed as to progress. (We'd strongly urge that everyone go out for a few minutes each day during the first week so responsibility is assumed by all members of the staff whose total presence signals to students, "We mean it.") Also, each teacher will be able to check on his/her own students and follow-up accordingly. This will mean inconvenience, giving up some of those precious minutes of free time for a short period, but the dividends from such sacrifice will give everyone more time, energy, and "peace" to do important things for the rest of the year.

24

Step IV: Reinforcement of Productive Behavior.

While the fun of being on a satisfying playground is a powerful reinforcer, some students will also need the social reinforcer of the approval of significant others. Teachers, aides/volunteers, and occasionally the principal, when on the yard, need to watch for and signal to students their recognition of appropriate behavior. ("You're really a good sport to accept the umpire's decision." "Wow, you're getting good at this game." "Even though you didn't want to stop when the bell rang, you did. You're really in charge of yourself!") The staff might begin their strategy to improve playground behavior with a letter to all parents telling of the plans for a safer, happier noon yard and letting them know that they will receive a letter from school *when* (not if), their child is doing well. A week later, a form letter (with the student's name written in) can go to parents commenting on their child's cooperation and good behavior. The results from a written reinforcer are amazing.

Notice that, at the beginning of this strategy, only positive reinforcers are used. Students who present problems will be helped ("Tom, what would be a better way to do that?" "Sally, the bell has rung; you need to stop playing"). Use of positive reinforcers plus help for offenders will bring most students "into the fold." After a week or two, for those students who are still having problems, the staff will need to determine which negative reinforcers to use with the few (you'll be surprised how few!) "sinners" that are left. Elimination from the yard for a day is a very normal consequence of inappropriate behavior and constitutes a negative reinforcer for most students. Whether the culprit is banished to an uninteresting spot inside the school or to his home at noon, depends on what is appropriate to the geography and the politics of the situation. On the following day, when the culprit returns to the yard, (s)he needs all the teacher help possible to successfully practice the correct behavior. (Remember, a student can't learn math by only having his problems marked wrong. Someone has to show him how to do it and then he must practice doing it correctly.)

The improvement of students' behavior from a systematic total staff strategy often is so dramatic that the staff concludes, "Thank goodness, that is done. Now we can get to more important teaching." Unfortunately, students, like linen closets, do not stay in order. After awhile, things begin to deteriorate and the job of "putting things in order" must be redone. This would be discouraging if improvement were not so quickly achieved the second time. Consequently, a time must be set

(1–3 months hence) to reevaluate, redesign, and *restaff* the next step in productive behavior on the yard.

The improvement of noon yard (the same strategy will work for recess periods and before and after school or for any other problem) is dependent on five factors:

1. Staff agreement on *specific* productive behaviors.
2. Staff design of a collaborative strategy for achieving that behavior.
3. Staff commitment of time to *teach* for (not just wish for) the improved behavior.
4. Systematic reinforcement by *all* staff members of the improved behavior whenever it occurs.
5. Occasional reemphasis, by the whole staff, to eliminate the inevitable "fall out" that occurs after a period of time, and to bring the behavior back to an acceptable state or raise it to a higher level.

For whatever behavior the staff has chosen for focus, remember that children will do well that which they are *taught* to do well. They can't be expected to do something well just because they've been told they should, any more than a first grader can be expected to know how to read because his teacher told him he should. While, at first inspection, learning to read or learning to play a game or learning to behave appropriately may seem very different, all those behaviors need deliberate, planned teaching with remediation to correct errors at the time they occur. If this help is given, most learners soon read well or behave appropriately without needing a teacher. This is the way all independence is achieved—not by admonition, but by teaching.

And that's our goal in education!

INCREASING STUDENTS' MOTIVATION TO LEARN

MEETING PLAN

Long Range Objective
Teachers will demonstrate proficiency in the application of professional knowledge and skill to promote increased motivation of learners.

Staff Meeting Objectives
Teachers will state the six factors which affect students' motivation to learn, that are subject to teacher control.

Teachers will give classroom and playground examples of use and abuse of each factor.

Each teacher will identify one student behavior or class behavior to improve through the use of factors which influence motivation.

Preparation for Staff Meeting
Teachers should have the opportunity to read the article on motivation on page 31 or read the reference or see one of the films listed on pages 29–30 before the staff meeting. If this is not possible, the meeting should begin with the principal or a designated member of the group presenting the material in these references or showing one of the films, clarifying and discussing each principle as it is presented. The time taken to present the content at the beginning of the meeting will mean that discussion of the six factors that affect motivation and the teachers plans to use those factors may extend into a second meeting. Sometimes this extension is desirable as it gives teachers time to "digest" what they have heard and translate their understanding into mature plans for action.

Staff Discussion
The discussion should stress:
1. Each factor in motivation is neither beneficial nor harmful in itself, it has the potential for either effect, depending on how it is used.

2. After listing all six variables on the chalkboard, each should be applied to the same problem, such as being late, not finishing work (example on page 36), sloppy writing, etc. In this way, the teachers will begin to develop a repertoire of responses to any one student behavior or class problem and will not settle on the use of just one factor.

3. Teachers also should generate examples of incorrect us of each factor and identify student behaviors which would signal them that concern or anxiety was too high, pleasant feeling tone wasn't working, all of a student's attention was directed to novelty and not to the learning, etc.

4. Teachers should be encouraged to volunteer examples of motivational problems from their own classroom for the group to discuss, thereby building reality and transfer probability into the meeting. However, beware of taking the worst problem in the school for discussion even though this may be cathartic. When teachers or anyone else is learning a new skill, they need to practice on simpler problems before they tackle the most difficult one.

The discussion should conclude with the assignment that each teacher will select one student or class behavior, try using what was discussed in the meeting, observe the results carefully and, at a future meeting, share successes or generate additional suggestions for students who haven't responded.

Follow-up

If there is not enough time at the initial meeting on motivation, discussion should be continued at a subsequent meeting scheduled as soon as possible in order to eliminate the fallout of forgetting and to bring additional meaning to the information. If the teachers have already done prior reading and leave the first meeting with adequate knowledge of the motivational variables, the follow-up meeting can be scheduled after a week or two. In the interim, the principal should continue to "prime the pump" with expressions of interest, classroom visits and participation in the teachers efforts.

At the subsequent meeting where teachers share their experiences, support must be focused on the effort the teacher has made and the integrity with which (s)he has used the motivational factors rather than the expectation of 100 percent success. Too many quick successes become suspect, for that is not the way most professional skills are acquired.

Principal's Responsibilities

The principal needs to practice the use of motivation theory with teachers, for they are the people for whose learning (s)he is responsible. This is a new role. It is easy to see what "ought to be done in the classroom" but, more difficult to apply those same principles of learning to the people for whose performance the principal is responsible. Lest using motivation theory on staff sounds like "manipulation," know that the principal is a powerful model in the school and when (s)he practices the theory (with labeling of what (s)he is doing), professional skills become more easily transmittable. "I am going to raise—lower your level of concern." "You should be pleased with this knowledge of results" indicates the principal is aware of, values, and is "practicing what (s)he preaches."

The principal also is a valuable resource to his teachers as (s)he lets children know (s)he is concerned about their performances, and as (s)he gives knowledge of results to the teacher, the student and to the parents. A note home will work wonders, particularly if it is positive (pleasant feeling tone) and gives knowledge of results ("Bill is really improving in his promptness—handwriting—number facts, etc.") or arouses interest ("Bill and I will let you know how much he has learned by next week").

In short, it is the principal's sophistication with, and use of principles of motivation that makes theory come alive for the staff and serves as the model for their productive use of motivational factors in the classroom.

Dividends

While motivation theory won't cure all the ills of education, it will go a long way towards increasing students' motivation to learn, teachers' motivation to increase their professional competency, parents motivation to support and augment the efforts of the school and the principal's motivation (and skill) to become an educational leader.

For additional information:

Book:
Hunter, Madeline. *Motivation Theory for Teachers*. California: TIP Publications, P.O. Box 514, El Segundo, California 90245. 1967

Films:

"Motivation Theory for Teachers." black and white. 30 minutes.

"Increasing Motivation." color. 30 minutes.

"Motivation and Reinforcement in the Classroom." color. 30 minutes.

SPECIAL PURPOSE FILMS
  26740 Latigo Shore Drive
  Malibu, California 90265

INCREASING MOTIVATION TO LEARN *

All of us are puzzled by the lack of motivation of some learners. Now we can learn how to do something about it.

Motivation is a state *within* a learner in the same way that hunger is a feeling within a person. No one can *make* a person hungry, but one can arrange conditions (the sight and smell of delicious food, or not permitting a person to have food) which will increase the probability of that person becoming hungry.

It is the same with motivation. You cannot motivate a learner, but you can arrange conditions that will increase the problelity of the motivation to learn becoming stronger.

There are all kinds of factors that influence motivation, the learner's parents, his previous teachers, the quality of his breakfast, whether or not his team won. You'll note that all of these "influences" have already happened and there is nothing that you can do to change those past events. You can explain motivation (or lack of it) by looking at the past, but if you want motivation to increase, you must focus on the present and make something happen *now* that will affect the student's intent to learn.

There are six factors which have a powerful effect on motivation: they are 1) concern, 2) feeling tone, 3) interest, 4) success, 5) knowledge of results and 6) extrinsic-intrinsic motivation. You can use each of these factors in your classroom.

1. *Concern.* Learners are motivated to do that which they're concerned about. "I don't care" can mean "I won't try."

   If concern is too high, it interferes with motivation because it may become "I'm afraid to try." Each of us has an optimal level of concern that motivates us to greater effort and higher performance. The athlete performs well when he is extremely concerned about excelling. Some people "go to pieces" when they become too anxious or concerned. Those people function better with lower levels of concern.

   Watch your learners to see what happens when you do something to raise their level of concern. Does "I will be there in three minutes to see how much you have done" spur on a reluctant learner, or disable him with too much anxiety? There is no one

*This is a brief summary of the content presented in *Motivation Theory for Teachers.* That book should be available as a reference, for examples, for extension of understanding and application of these concepts.

right thing to do, it varies with each learner. Don't let a learner remain unconcerned. ("I missed them all again"—big joke!) On the other hand, reassure an over-anxious learner ("Don't worry if you missed some, we're all having trouble"). These decisions on your part are what make teaching a profession.

2. *Feeling tone.* What you do can make the feeling tone pleasant, unpleasant or neutral. For example you can say:

"You write such interesting stories, I'm anxious to read this one."

"That story must be finished before you're excused for lunch."

"If you aren't finished, don't worry, there'll be plenty of time later."

The first statement expresses pleasant feeling tone which should increase the motivation of the learner to finish his story. The second statement expresses unpleasant feeling tone which also may increase the motivation of the learner to finish but it can have undesirable side effects (he learns to hate story writing). The third statement indicates neutral feeling tone which has little or no effect on motivation.

So, by all means, increase motivation to learn by making school pleasant. If that doesn't work and you must become a little unpleasant, *make sure you return to pleasant feeling tone as soon as the learner has performed.* ("It's a really good story, Bill, I'm glad I insisted you stay to finish it.") Don't fall into the trap of delivering a "lecture" once the student has performed. ("It's about time you finished.") Leave him with a pleasant feeling so he'll want to "do it again." Neutral feeling tone is helpful when you decide this is "not the time" for you or that student. ("Let's skip it for now.")

3. *Interest.* It is obvious that we are more motivated to learn something that interests us. The important thing to remember is that interest, like reading, is learned, not something a student is born with. A skilled teacher, aide or volunteer can develop students' interest in two ways: a) by making the learning more meaningful to the learner; b) by making the learning vivid or different from what the student usually experiences or is expecting.

All of us are interested in ourselves, so inclusion of something about a learner along with the content to be learned is meaningful and very interest evoking. ("Bill, suppose you made five home runs every day for six days. How many home runs would you

32

have made?") This same motivation occurs if you place a new word to be learned in a sentence with the learner's name ("Bill *earned* five dollars by helping his father.") The possibilities are limited only by your creativity.

A second way to generate interest is to do things in a different or novel way. Change some things in the room or bring in something different, use "pen names" in creative writing, make a puzzle or game out of a necessary drill. Your initiative and creativity will help you to make assignments more interesting. If school is a drag—change something! Make sure, however, that most of your effort goes into teaching. Don't put so much of your time and energy into novel gimmicks that you haven't any time and energy left for helping the student *learn* once his interest is aroused.

4. *Success.* A learner's motivation increases as his success increases. When a teacher, aide or volunteer wonders, "Why doesn't Bill work on spelling? He knows he has trouble with it," she has answered her own question. You can make a student's success more probable by setting the task at the right level of difficulty for him. Make sure that the assignment is not too difficult for some, they'll give up. The ones for whom the assignment is too easy will quit of boredom. If *with some effort* a student can be successful, he's more motivated to try because he experiences and enjoys his own strength and competence. The skilled teacher has assignments of different degrees of difficulty for different children (not necessarily different for each child). Diagnosis of learners, to be sure they're working on the right level of difficulty, and the use of principles of learning° will enable each learner to become more successful.

5. *Knowledge of Results.* The answer to "How am I doing" is highly motivational, for it lets a learner know when he's right or what he needs to change. He needs this information *while* he's learning—not the next day, the next week, or at the end of the year. When you return papers, comments are much more effective in increasing motivation than are grades. "A good beginning, can you make the ending as exciting?" gives a learner a lot more knowlege of results than the grade of "B."

Having a learner check his answers as he's doing the assignment or immediately after he's finished, increases his motivation when he's successful and also builds in correction at the crucial time if he's having trouble. The most effective learning is accomplished

°See TIP Publications listed at end of chapter.

33

when you make sure that the student knows when he has done well or, when he hasn't, what needs to be corrected. This is true in learning new patterns of behavior as well as in academic learning. Examples of giving a student knowledge of results might be:

"Tom, you did a great job of starting to work, now you need to let me know when you've finished the first part."

"Sally, you really played well today, you're learning to be a good sport."

"Put your thumb up if what I say is something that could have really happened."

Often you need to ask the learners to evaluate their own performance and answer the question for themselves "How did I do today on this job?" Then you encourage the intrinsic motivation of the learner supplying his own knowledge of results.

6. *Intrinsic vs. Extrinsic Motivation.* Intrinsic motivation is developed when the activity or learning itself is the reward for effort. Extrinsic motivation exists when the student makes an effort to learn in order to gain something else such as status, approval, grades, to get it over with, or to avoid unpleasant consequences. Don't expect your learners to always learn only for the joy of learning. While that may be educational Utopia, we seldom achieve it. You and I are not intrinsically motivated to do dishes, get up in the morning, turn in those (adjective deleted) reports and there's very little intrinsic motivation in our teaching when we're tired on a windy rainy Friday afternoon.

The more a learner is interested in and successful with his learning, the more the process of learning will become it's own reward. In the meantime, use extrinsic motivators such as, "You did a great job, you should be proud of yourself," "Let's see how much better you can do today than you did last week," (rather than competing with someone else), recording new words so a student can see how many he has learned, a complimentary note to take home. All of these are more productive and emotionally healthful motivators than report cards, charts where everyone's scores are exposed or odious comparisons between students of different abilities. "You did that so well you should feel very good about yourself" is a productive and well deserved reward for performance.

Members of your school staff will be saying just that about each other, as they report their successes in applying the six factors that increase students' motivation to learn.

34

For additional information:

Books:

Hunter, Madeline. *Motivation Theory for Teachers*. TIP Publications. P.O. Box 514, El Segundo, California 90245, 1967.

Hunter, Madeline. *Reinforcement Theory for Teachers*. TIP Publications. P.O. Box 514, El Segundo, California 90245. 1967.

Hunter, Madeline. *Retention Theory for Teachers*. TIP Publications. P.O. Box 514, El Segundo, California 90245. 1967.

Hunter, Madeline. *Teach More—Faster!* TIP Publications. P.O. Box 514, El Segundo, California 90245. 1969.

Hunter, Madeline. *Teach for Transfer*. TIP Publications. P.O. Box 514, El Segundo, California 90245. 1971.

Films:

Hunter, Madeline. Part II "Motivation Theory for Teachers." black and white. 28 minutes.

"Increasing Students' Motivation to Learn." color. 30 minutes.

"Motivation and Reinforcement in the Classroom." color. 30 minutes.

SPECIAL PURPOSE FILMS
26740 Latigo Shore Drive
Malibu, California 90265

USING MOTIVATION THEORY

In response to a student's statement, "Do I have to do it?"

Concern	Raise	"Yes, it must be finished before you leave."
	Lower	"I can understand the way you feel. I'll help you do the first one. Great. Can you do the next one by yourself or do you want help?"
Feeling Tone	Pleasant	"This will be easy for you, you're very good at it."
	Unpleasant	"You know what my answer will be."
	Neutral	"It's up to you."

Interest	"If you were the teacher and were teaching me how to do it, what would you have me do first?" (Assuming being teacher was desirable to that student.)
Success	"You did the last ones just perfectly, I'll bet you can have these done in just a few minutes and they'll all be right." (If that's likely.)
Knowledge of Results	"You have the first one all correct except—. Now it's perfect. I'll come back in a minute and check the next one."
Extrinsic	"As soon as you're finished you may choose what you want to do."
Intrinsic	"You'll find that you're getting so skilled these are fun to do."

DO'S AND DON'TS IN USING MOTIVATION THEORY

1. Do build a learner's productive concern about his learning.

   "Let's see if you can beat your yesterday's record."

   "I'll be back in a minute to see how you're doing."

   "We'll come back to it later to see if you remember."

2. Do use pleasant feeling tone.

   "I'll bet you can learn them."

   "You're really a fast learner."

   "You're fun to teach."

3. Do make examples interesting and meaningful.

   "Suppose you made five home runs everyday for four days, how many home runs would you have made?"

   "If you got $5 for your birthday and your grandmother said, I'll give you three times that much how much money would your grandmother give you?"

4. Do see that a learner experiences success.

   "Let's count how many new words you've learned."

1. Don't build so much concern the learner can't concentrate on the task.

   "If you don't get them *all* right, you'll have to stay after school."

   "This is the last chance you'll have for help."

   "Your whole grade depends on this."

2. Don't use pleasant feeling tone when it isn't working.

   "Even though you're not trying very hard, I'm here to help you."

3. Don't make things so vivid the learner thinks more about them than he does about the learning.

   "Suppose three monsters came in your room every night . . ."

   "Suppose you got three time $5 from your grandmother, what are all the things you'd like to buy?"

   "I'll time you with this stop watch. Have you ever seen a stop-watch work?

4. Don't have the job so hard he can't possibly do it or so easy he doesn't have to try.

   "I know you've never done

"You see you got them all right."
"I just can't catch you."

one this hard but try to figure it out."
"You always get these right. Let's do them again."

5. Do give the learner specific knowledge of results.
   "Your spelling is correct but be careful your "i's" don't look like "e's."
   "Your surprise ending made your story just great."

5. Don't give only general information.
   "That's o.k."
   "It's a "B" paper."
   "I put a check on your paper to show you I've seen it."

6. Do use extrinsic motivation when the learner has no intrinsic motivation to learn a particular thing. After successful learning many things become intrinsically motivated.
   "Your dad will be so surprised to find you know this."
   "Finish it so you can be one of the first out to recess."

6. Don't negotiate or bribe to get a child to learn.
   "If you do this, I will ..." tempts him to consider whether it is worth it to put forth the effort. "Finish this so you can ..." makes it clear the job is to be done but there will be pleasant consequences.

ADDITIONAL MOTIVATIONAL PHRASES

Concern:

I'll help you with the first part and then I'll come back to see how you're doing.

As soon as your paper is finished, you may go out for recess.

I saw what a good job you did in spelling yesterday, I know you will do well again today.

Good for you, I couldn't catch you on that page. Look at this next page and I'll bet I still won't be able to catch you on any words.

You will need to listen carefully when I read this story so when I finish, you will know the answer to some questions.

Feeling Tone:

Pleasant:

You have done such a good job, let's put your paper on the bulletin board.

I am writing 'good thinking' on this paper because you have done so well.

Let's show this paper to the principal so (s)he can see how hard you worked—that's why you got all the answers correct.

Unpleasant:

I'll work with you during free choice time and see what's giving you trouble with your spelling.

You need to show that you can do that page without any more help.

You need to do these problems at home and check with me tomorrow so I know you've learned how.

If you waste time now, you'll need to finish during your playtime.

Interest:

You like football, Joe, so tell me: If the home team made 2 touch-downs and a field goal,—how many points would that be? The opponents made 1 touchdown and 2 field goals, how many points did they make? Who won? By how many points?

Let's take some of the words you're learning and write a story about YOU using these words.

Knowledge of Results:

You got everything just right!

You answered all the questions about the first half of the chapter correctly, but you will need to read the last half more carefully to correct the answers to these questions.

You know your addition facts but you still need to work on your subtraction facts.

Your spaces between words are too small. You need to make them bigger.

The paragraph you wrote was interesting, your choice of words good, the punctuation just right. Now you need to work on your handwriting so it will be easier to read.

Success:

This whole list of words looks like a lot to learn, but if you work on just a few of the words each day you'll know them all by Friday. Let's mark off the words to learn each day.

You read that story with no mistakes. Here's a new book because you're ready for one that is more difficult.

Now I'll read a page. You be 'my teacher' and fill in the words when I stop.

Extrinsic:

You need to learn your 6 times tables perfectly before you can work with that new _____.

You've learned to work without disturbing the group, you may have free choice.

As soon as you're finished, you may choose a partner and play this game.

Put a mark on this chart each time your math paper is finished on time. Five marks mean you may choose a special activity.

Intrinsic:

Yes, you may share your book on rock collecting that you enjoyed so much.

I see the subject was so interesting you read additional books beyond your assignment.

You're having fun making up your own problems in math, aren't you?

EXTENDING STUDENTS' THINKING

MEETING PLAN

Long Range Objectives

Teachers will demonstrate proficiency in developing learning opportunities that extend students' thinking into application, analysis, synthesis, and evaluation of material that has been learned.

Students will demonstrate higher level thinking skills.

Meeting Objectives

Teachers will state the six levels of the cognitive domain and identify questions and activities at each level.

Teachers will take a specific activity (holiday, reading or social studies assignment) and generate questions and activities at each level of the taxonomy which will be appropriate for their own students.

Preparation for Staff Meeting

Teachers should have the opportunity to read the section on Extending Students' Thinking page 45. If this is not possible, the principal or a designated staff member should begin the meeting with a presentation of the material or show one of the films listed on page 44, stopping to clarify each level of the taxonomy as it is presented.

Presentation of the content at the beginning of the meeting will probably necessitate continuing discussion and generating examples at a subsequent meeting. This is desirable as it gives teachers the opportunity to examine their classroom assignments to determine whether students are spending too much time on the level of recall and comprehension or if students are expected to do high level thinking without the prior information or understanding that is required.

Discussion

After teachers have achieved understanding of the levels of the taxonomy through discussion and the presentation of many examples by the leader, they should apply their understanding to new material. If the meeting is scheduled close to any holiday, teachers should generate activities which will move students from stereotypical activities into creative assignments that will challenge student's thinking (examples on page 49).

It also is productive to bring sufficient copies of frequently used materials so each teacher may use one. (Weekly readers, news magazines, social studies books or readers.) These materials should be at a middle grade level so teachers of younger or older students can adjust the ideas to their level. Each teacher can scan a story or article and generate assignments at every level of thinking.

The staff should be divided into small groups (3–5) for discussion, and contribute their suggestions to the total staff at the end of the meeting. Each group may work on the same material or groups may select the material of their interest. Both plans will give exciting results.

At the end of the meeting, teachers should be encouraged to examine their subsequent classroom assignments to determine if they are expecting students to be creative and do high level thinking without the necessary foundation of information and understanding or if they are expecting only the memorization of factual material and not requiring its application to the students' own lives.

It is important to stress that, like all learners, the teachers must first possess information about and understand the levels of thinking. Then they must apply this understanding by diagnosing their learners (analysis) and developing appropriate assignments (synthesis). Finally, they must evaluate the success of the activity and make a judgment of which learners are successful and why. That is why teaching is such a complex profession. It always requires the level of evaluation and judgment.

Follow-up

Facility with systematically using the levels of the taxonomy is not achieved in one meeting or one month, but must be the subject of continuing focus throughout the school year. With practice, teachers automate their own thinking in this area and easily generate assignments at the appropriate level.

Asking teachers for suggestions before holidays or special events and then compiling and duplicating their ideas for use by the entire staff, can be a periodic practice and reminder of the importance of higher level thinking.

Principal's Responsibilities

Frequent, brief visits to classrooms can give the principal significant feedback as to the level of thinking being required of students. (S)he must be alert, however, to whether or not that level is appropriate for *those* students *at that time*. Often, the erroneous assumption is made that younger students should be working on information and older students at higher levels of thinking. The student's age is not the critical factor. If students possess information and understanding in an area, they should be doing higher level thinking in that area. If the content is new, regardless of students' age, they should be acquiring information and demonstrating that they comprehend what they are learning.

The principal should also be aware that staff meetings can only give information and make it easier to comprehend and apply that information. Higher levels of thinking required to translate teaching skills into action patterns in the classroom occur within the classroom. Consequently, observation is the only completely valid evidence of application of the staff meeting content in a classroom situation.

To enlist the support of a parent body, it is important that they have information about thinking skills which they can understand and apply at home. Consequently, it is suggested that a night meeting, which involves fathers, be devoted to Bloom's Taxonomy. Parents will enjoy knowing how the teachers are working to extend their child's thinking and will zestfully practice trying to generate activities at all levels of the Taxonomy when they are divided into small groups. The meeting plan for teachers can be replicated for parents with extremely productive results.

Dividends

"Extending students' thinking" is a concept with which teachers, parents and taxpayers will agree. As each of these groups become knowledgeable about how to achieve this goal rather than wishing for or mandating it, students' thinking and school support grow together.

A second, equally important dividend is the increase in interest and effort on students' part as assignments become more provocative and challenging.

The third and most important dividend is that students are practicing a skill which they need daily and which they will increasingly need throughout their lives as they make decisions, resolve issues, and become competent, satisfied, contributing members of society.

For additional information:

Films:

"Objectives in the Cognitive Domain." black and white. 30 minutes.

"Extending Students' Thinking." color. 30 minutes.

"Reading a Story to Extending Thinking." color. 30 minutes.

"Reading for Analysis." black and white. 30 minutes.

SPECIAL PURPOSE FILMS
  26740 Latigo Shore Drive
  Malibu, California 90265

EXTENDING STUDENTS' THINKING

Extending students' skills in complex thinking, as well as developing their ability to apply that thinking process to the creative solution of problems, has become an important goal of education. In spite of educators' dedication to this goal, many school assignments involve only recalling information and being tested for knowledge of facts (names, dates, number facts, etc.). Having information is important, but the students need the opportunity, as well as the responsibility for using that information in life situations and in creative ways. Several years ago, Dr. Benjamin Bloom of the University of Chicago developed a taxonomy or classification system of the cognitive domain in order to identify the levels of thinking demanded of students. This classification system makes it possible to deliberately develop school assignments and independent activities that enable students to practice extending their information into higher and more creative levels of thinking.

Bloom's six levels of cognition (thinking), *greatly simplified* are:

1. Knowledge: *Recall or location of information.* This is the most common type of classroom assignment. An example of this level of thinking is the factual question (What did Columbus do? How much is 5 x 25? What happened in the story?). The information is remembered or the answer to the question can be located and does not need to be interpreted or inferred. Activities at this level provide the student with *information* which he can use to generate more complex thinking. There is nothing wrong with teaching facts, they are essential to all higher levels of thinking. But don't stop there, enable students to use those facts in more elaborate or creative ways.

2. *Comprehension or Understanding.* This level of thinking requires that students *understand* the facts they are learning, not merely recall or parrot information. "Why" and "how" questions may test understanding providing the student explains in his own words and doesn't merely repeat something he has read or heard. "Give an example" or "Say it in a different way" are ways of checking a student's understanding.

Examples of activities which require understanding are:

a. Draw a picture that would go with the beginning of the story, one that would show what happened in the middle of the story and one that happened at the end.

45

b. Give an example of something the boy did that showed he was dependable.

c. Explain what you are doing while you are working the problem.

d. How do you think the boy in the story felt? (Providing it doesn't tell this in the story.)

These first two levels of thinking, possession of information and understanding that information, constitute the foundation on which all complex thinking is built. A learner cannot do creative or high level thinking without this foundation. (It is impossible to make judgments about democracy and socialism unless there is understanding of what each is.) Again, the important function of teaching is to start with the foundation but encourage the student to build on his understanding and extend his thinking.

3. *Application.* The third level of cognition is the beginning of creative thinking. Application includes activities where the student applies what he has learned to a situation which is new to him rather than one where he remembers the answers.

Examples of application activities are:

a. Solve word problems in math.

b. Apply a generalization or principle to a new situation. Examples: "Which of these imaginary animals could live in intense cold?" (Assuming that the student has learned that a warm blooded animal has to have some protective covering.) "On this map, locate the most likely places for cities." (The student had to apply what he has learned about the location of cities such as: close to a major trade route, where water is accessible, etc.).

c. What might Goldilocks do if she came to your house and you weren't home?

d. If you treated him as you would like to be treated, what would you do?

The ability to apply what has been learned to a new situation is a very important goal in education for we cannot possibly provide practice in all the situations the student will encounter throughout life.

4. *Analysis.* The fourth level of cognition requires that the student "take apart" his information to examine or work with the different parts. This level of thinking requires the ability to categorize, which is man's unique intellectual technique to reduce the complexity of his world. The ability to perceive similarity in different things and difference in similar things requires the skill of *analysis*.

46

Examples are:

a. Tell five ways the boy in the story is the same as you and five ways he is different.

b. List the words in the story that describe appearance and those that describe movement.

c. What were the three main ideas of the story?

d. How was Magellan the same as an astronaut? How was he different?

When students have to examine information and assign it to a prescribed category, they are operating at the level of analysis. A higher level of thinking is required if they have to create new categories in order to organize the information. Creation or invention of new categories constitutes synthesis or the fifth level of cognition. An analogy would be the determination of where material belonged and filing of that material in an organized filing system (analysis) or the creation of a new filing system in order to organize the material. (synthesis)

5. *Synthesis.* This level of thinking requires that a student create or invent something; a generalization, picture, poem, story, organizational scheme, category, hypothesis. Synthesis requires the bringing together of more than one piece of information, idea, concept or set of skills.

Examples of activities requiring synthesis are:

a. A creative endeavor in the arts, a picture, a new melody, an additional stanza or a new poem or dance, etc.

b. Creating a story based on what might have happened if Red Riding Hood had met only a mouse in the forest.

c. Writing an original story.

d. Developing a hypothesis.

e. Designing an experiment that would test that hypothesis.

6. *Evaluation or Judgment.* Judgments are made when clearly there is more than one possible point of view and the difference between a judgment and a guess is that the student can give reasons to support the judgment he makes. This is the highest level of thinking because in an evaluative judgment or opinion there is no right or wrong answer until you consider the evidence that is used to support that answer or conclusion. The person's judgment is considered valid when there is evidence to support it. A judgment should be supported by the answer to "why do you think so?" or "how can you tell?"

47

Examples of activities on an evaluation or judgment level are:

a. Which would have been more difficult, to be Daniel Boone or Columbus? Why do you think so?
b. What should we serve at our party? Why?
c. Under what conditions might a person be justified in not telling the truth? Why?
d. Which solution is better? Why?

To ask learners to make judgments and support them with data is to require thinking on the highest level of cognition. To ask less is to deny students the opportunity to practice becoming intelligent decision makers.

These six categories of thinking (knowledge, comprehension, application, analysis, synthesis and evaluation) provide a framework for designing appropriate activities to extend students' thinking. Remember, however, that students must have information which they understand *before* they can use it in new and creative ways. A student can't be creative until he has acquired the skill or information necessary to that creativity.

It is not critical that you be able to identify or label the precise level of cognition for each learning activity. The important idea is to *stimulate students to think beyond recalling and understanding information*. Once those levels have been achieved, encourage students to use their information in problem solving and creative endeavors. Plan activities that require the student to identify similarities and differences, categorize information, speculate "what would happen if - - -," compare and contrast others and themselves, create a new beginning or ending.

When you ask students to give an opinion or make a judgment about a person, situation or idea, have them cite the evidence which will support their judgment so it's not merely a haphazard guess or recall of something they have been told.

Make sure, however, that the student *has* the information necessary to do creative thinking. Do not ask him to give opinions about something he doesn't understand. Questions such as "Which is the better form of government?" "What do you think about this interracial crisis?" "What do you think about this political figure?" or other complex questions, may encourage him merely to parrot what he has heard from others when he does not have the information or understand it well enough to form his own "thinking opinion."

As you practice developing these activities for students, you'll be amazed and delighted to find how much you have extended your own thinking.

EXAMPLES FOR EXTENDING THINKING

Here are sample questions and activities for familiar stories. See if you can think of additional ones at the higher levels.

THE PLEDGE OF ALLEGIANCE

Recall
1. Say the Pledge.

Comprehension
1. Say in your own words (not just give a synonym) or give examples of what these words mean: "pledge allegiance" "indivisible" "liberty and justice for all."
2. Write your own definitions of those words.
3. Paraphrase the Pledge.

Application
1. What does liberty and justice on the playground mean?
2. To what other organizations and people do you own allegiance?
3. What else is indivisible in the same sense as our nation?

Analysis
1. What parts of the Pledge refer to you and what parts to the nation?
2. Compare the Pledge to another pledge (Scouts, etc.), how are they the same and how different?
3. What elements do all pledges have?

Synthesis
1. Write a pledge for your family that all members would be willing to sign.
2. Write a class pledge (school, neighborhood, community, club, etc.).

Evaluation
1. Should every nation have a pledge? Support your position.
2. Should every one say the Pledge? Support your position.
3. Should the Pledge be said everyday? Support your position.
4. What would improve the Pledge? Why?

VALENTINE'S DAY

Possession of information
1. What are some things people put on valentines?

Comprehension
1. Tell about St. Valentine in your own words.
2. What do the symbols on valentines represent?

Application
1. What could be another occasion for which we might designate a special day and send cards (not one we have now)?
2. What symbols would we use for that day?

Analysis
1. What kinds of comic valentines are funny and what kinds hurt people's feelings?
2. How many different ways might valentines be sorted into categories?

Synthesis
1. Make a comic valentine that would make *you* laugh and one that would make you angry or unhappy.
2. Make a valentine for your friend with none of the typical symbols or words.

Evaluation
1. Should we spend time on Valentine's day at school? Support your answer.
2. What would be the best way to observe Valentine's Day? Why?

RED RIDING HOOD

Possession of information
1. What did the wolf say his big eyes were for?
2. Where did she meet the wolf?

Comprehension
1. Tell what a hood is, in your own words.
2. What kind of a girl was Red Riding Hood?

Higher level thinking
1. What did Red Riding Hood's mother do that was kind?
2. Which parts of the story could have really happened?
3. Which parts are make believe?
4. What do you think the wolf would have done if grandma had not been sick?
5. How is Red Riding Hood's mother like yours? In what ways is she different?
6. Make a picture with one thing that is different from the story and we'll see if we're good enough detectives to find it.

THREE LITTLE PIGS

Possession of information
1. What did the pigs use to build houses?
2. What did the pigs say when the wolf wanted in?

Comprehension
1. How did they finally get rid of the wolf?
2. Why didn't the brick house blow down?

Higher level thinking
1. If there were no stove, what else might the third pig have used to get rid of the wolf?
2. How can you tell it's a make believe story?
3. Make up a story about another adventure with the three pigs.
4. Draw a picture about a different ending.
5. In what way is the Three Little Pigs like the story of Red Riding Hood?

THE STORY OF COLUMBUS

Possession of information
1. Where was Columbus going?
2. How did Columbus get the money for his voyage?

Comprehension
1. What did the sailors depend on to make their ships go?
2. What did they use to guide them on course?

51

Higher level thinking
1. List some of the things that would make a voyage difficult.
2. How did Columbus seek help when there was nothing he or the sailors could do?
3. When Columbus returned, how would the celebration be like one we might have for astronauts today? How would it be different?
4. What kind of a man do you think Columbus was and what makes you think so?
5. Who was braver, Columbus or an astronaut?

DESIGNING EFFECTIVE PRACTICE

MEETING PLAN

Long Range Objective
Students' practice will be effective in accomplishing learning, and will be economical in time expended.

Staff Meeting Objectives
Teachers will discuss factors that contribute to effective practice.

Teachers will generate examples of how these factors can be incorporated into classroom practice periods.

Teachers will incorporate these factors in daily classroom experiences, monitor the learning results, and produce increased student proficiency.

Preparation for Staff Meeting
Teachers should have the opportunity before the staff meeting, to read the article on practice on page 58. If this is not possible, the meeting should begin with the principal or a designated member of the group presenting the material or showing the film "Improving Practice" so there is a common knowledge base for group discussion. In this case, the discussion will probably extend into a second meeting which should be scheduled as soon as possible.

Teachers also might be asked, before this meeting, to identify some content or activity in their classroom that needs practice and have that information ready, verbally or in writing, to use as an example for group focus and discussion during the staff meeting. Using a "real life" example will more nearly ensure transfer of the strategies developed by staff discussion to classroom application.

Discussion

The discussion should emphasize examples of the 3 M's of practice and answers to the questions:

1. How much of a task should be practiced at one time?
2. How long should the practice periods be?
3. How often should the practice periods be scheduled?
4. How will the student know how well he is doing?

It is more vivid to list only the key words on the chalkboard.

3 M's

Meaning
Modeling
Monitoring

Questions:

1. How much?
2. How long?
3. How often?
4. How well?

Teachers should identify activities that require practice in their classroom. The group can suggest several ways to ensure meaning in what is being practiced and then answer the four questions in relation to each activity. Examples of common violations of the answers to these questions also should be elicited (such as practicing all 100 number facts, too many spelling words, an hour on the same activity, not checking papers for a week, etc.). By contrasting productive and unproductive techniques, each teacher will be encouraged to examine his own classroom practice.

In addition to the importance of *meaning* in eliminating the need for so much practice, *knowledge of results* (knowing how well he is doing) is also a critical factor. Teachers should discuss techniques and materials that give the student *immediate knowledge of results as to whether his practice is correct* and, if it is not, what is wrong. If he has made mistakes, additional opportunities should be provided on that same day for the student to practice the correct response, *not* wait until the next day to correct errors.

Examples of securing knowledge of results:

1. In the staff meeting each teacher will list the four generalizations which answer the questions that should be considered before sched-

54

uling practice (how much? how long? how often? and how well?).
Then teachers might check the results with the person sitting next
to him/her. The correct answers with examples should be identified for the total group so each teacher can check the accuracy
of her/his own answers.

2. The student will be checked or check him/herself on flash cards
(number facts, sight vocabulary) until (s)he identifies five or less
that (s)he does not know. (S)he will practice those until (s)he knows
them. Then the practiced facts should be mixed in with a few
already known facts to determine if (s)he still knows them when
they are imbedded in a longer series. These principles are violated
when a student goes through a long series of facts only looking
at the answers of the missed or unknown ones and then proceeding
without coming back again and again until (s)he is sure (s)he can
give the correct response for previous errors.

3. The student will take a pretest in spelling to identify the words
(s)he does not know. (S)he will get *immediate* knowledge of results
of correct response and errors, and will practice five or less (*not
more!*) words (s)he does not know and be re-checked *at that time*
by the teacher or a fellow student to determine whether they
are learned. At a later time (not immediately after (s)he has studied
the first group of word or (s)he will "braid" the learning into
additional errors (s)he will practice the next few words needed and
be checked on them *plus* the first group of learned words to see
if (s)he has retained those previously studied. If (s)he has forgotten
some of the first group or not learned some of the second group,
those words become the focus of the third study period. (*S)he
will not* proceed to additional words until (s)he has demonstrated
retention of the words already studied (not for discipline, or pun-
ishment, or shame, but for effective learning!).

An important part of every practice period is making sure that it
is made explicit to the learners, a) why they are practicing, b) effective
ways to make that practice pay higher learning dividends, and c) ways
to evaluate the results of practice so the learners know whether additional practice is needed.

At staff meetings, teachers can practice *making their learning about
practice* more meaningful and vivid if they role play, conducting short
intense practice periods with their fellow teachers to demonstrate techniques which each teacher then can modify and adapt to his/her own

classroom practice periods. The subject for practice can be academic content which is useful to teachers or some of the theory taught in this book.

Follow-up

It is suggested that an additional meeting be held so teachers can report back to the group on the practice generalizations they have "practiced" in their classrooms, those which were successful and those which didn't seem to work. Suggestions for improving the latter should be solicited from the group.

Other principles of learning from *Teach More—Faster!* (listed on page 65) which will reduce the need for practice can be introduced and discussed at a subsequent meeting. Again teachers should generate examples of use and abuse of each principle and suggest ways of incorporating them into classroom practice. The subject of practice can easily become the focus of several staff or grade level meetings.

Principal's Responsibilities

The material from this meeting is crucial for a principal's planning of inservice staff meetings. At a deliberate and conscious level, (s)he must incorporate the generalizations about practice in all the meetings. Meetings in this book are designed around one meaningful principle of learning. Practice on the content of the meeting should be massed during the initial staff meeting that deals with that content. During the week following, the principal should "practice" that content with the staff in lunchroom conversations, classroom observations or brief visits, casual encounters and scheduled conferences, always making the interaction meaningful by dealing with situations that are currently occurring with students or situations within the classroom and school.

The principal should give knowledge of results by positive comments, written and oral whenever (s)he sees a teacher using the principles of practice in a classroom and give suggestions of application of practice theory when students are encountering difficulty. The principal might open a subsequent staff meeting by describing some good examples of practice (s)he has seen without naming the teacher in whose room (s)he saw it. That teacher recognizes the teaching strategy and is positively reinforced for it but no one is embarrassed.

The principal is responsible for modeling distributed practice by incorporating the content of all previous meetings, where that content is applicable, in the current meeting, or situation. Often the temptation exists to breathe a sigh of relief when something is learned and then to forget it. Unfortunately, if the principal "forgets it" so will the teachers. Unless principles of learning are identified in each situation when they occur, they will remain an interesting topic of conversation in meetings but will not become a part of daily classroom experience.

"Practice what the meetings teach" is a critical responsibility of the principal.

Dividends

By making practice periods shorter and more effective, hours and hours of time will be saved which then can be devoted to some of the things "we never have time for." Art, music, social studies, discussions, pursuit of individual interests, drama, class meetings, etc., all those activities that teachers know are valuable yet which consume time the teacher feels she should spend on the 3 R's, can become the focus in the time which no longer is consumed by the ineffectual ritual of "just do it again." Well designed, short, intense, meaningful practice periods will result in more efficient and effective learning which is longer remembered and will release additional time for other important learning activities.

EFFECTIVE PRACTICE*

"Practice makes perfect," is not necessarily so. Performance can be improved or it can become worse as the result of practice. It all depends on *how* a person practices. There are ways of achieving effective learning with no practice whatsoever** and those ways should be considered before time is devoted to practice which is not necessary.

When students practice, there are basic principles that should guide that practice so significant improvement occurs with each practice period. As a result, not nearly so many practice periods will be needed. To achieve maximum learning gains with minimal time devoted to practice is one important goal of teaching.

Before a new skill is practiced, the teacher must provide for the "3 M's" that proceed a student's assuming responsibility for his/her own practice. The "3 M's" of practice are *meaning, modeling and monitoring.*

Meaning

Understanding the meaning of what is being practiced will significantly reduce the amount of time needed to learn. An obvious example is the amount of time it takes to learn to say ten nonsense syllables vs. the time needed to learn to say ten familiar words. If those ten words constitute a meaningful sentence ("You will receive ten dollars if you remember this sentence"), no practice at all will be necessary.

The important thing to remember is that meaning is not inherent in the material itself but the meaning exists in the relationship of the material to the learner's knowledge and past experience. Computer language would not be meaningful to a person who had no knowledge and experience in that area. In the same way, adults are sometimes baffled by "teen talk."

It is the responsibility of the teacher to build the bridge of meaning between what is to be practiced and the knowledge and experience of the particular learners who will be practicing. Spelling words should be translated into a sentence related to *those* learners ("Because you are working hard and paying attention and getting your work done, you are *diligent* students"). Math problems also should be translated into meaning for the learner rather than being merely exercises in

---

*Practice is considered to be "doing it again" in about the same way.
**See Hunter, Madeline. *Teach More—Faster!* for variables that make practice less necessary.

computation. (7 x 6 becomes, "If you got a part time job and earned $7.00 a day for 6 days, how much money would you have?")

To test whether the student really understands the meaning (rather than merely nodding agreement), it is necessary for students to make-up sentences, problems or give examples which incorporate the meaning. ("Give me a problem where you would need to multiply by 6," "What would you do to show your mother you are diligent?") When the student can generate an example rather than merely repeating one he has heard before, (s)he understands the material.

All practice periods, whether they are for new learning or to develop speed and fluency with familiar material, should begin with a check to make sure the material is meaningful in terms of the students' knowledge and past experience.

Modeling

A student's first experience with material makes a vivid learning impact; so teachers must make sure the impression is accurate. Consequently, the student should always begin with a good model. Usually the best way to ensure the correctness of the model is for the teacher to demonstrate the response the student is to practice. Whether it is a spelling word, a sentence, an arithmatic problem, writing a letter, or a paragraph, the teacher or an *accurate* student should model "how it should be."

Only when the student has already achieved reasonable accuracy in his response and is practicing to develop greater speed and fluency can this modeling step be omitted.

Monitoring

Next in importance to seeing the correct model is the necessity for the students' first practice responses to be as accurate as possible, for these responses are occuring at the critical initial stage in learning. If an error is practiced at the beginning of learning, it is much more difficult to eliminate than when that mistake occurs later in practice. Consequently, it is essential that the teacher carefully supervise the beginning practice of students so correct responses are encouraged and any error is caught and corrected as soon as possible.

Students should not independently practice new or unfamiliar content until the teacher's monitoring has indicated there is high probability that the practice will be reasonably correct.

All practice is for the purpose of making the student proficient and independent. When (s)he has developed reasonable comfort, accuracy, speed, and fluency with whatever is being practiced, (s)he no longer needs the teacher. Providing for the "3 M's" of meaning, modeling and monitoring at the beginning of practice of new material will immeasurably speed up this process. After meaning and correct responses are already established, the student can be responsible for his/her own practice without monitoring and modeling, and with only occasional checks for meaning.

There are four fundamentad questions that must be considered in order to plan an effective practice period. They are:

1. How much of a task should be practiced in one practice period?
2. How long should that practice period be?
3. How close together should those practice periods be scheduled?
4. How will the learner know how well he is doing?

To answer each of those questions, we need to look at some basic principles that have been validated by research.

1. How much of a task should be practiced in one practice period? The psychological generalization that guides teaching is: *The smallest amount of a task that retains maximum meaning is all that should be practiced at one time.*

Common sense would tell us this. We would not attempt to learn a long poem all at once. We would learn it one stanza at a time or even work on just a few lines of that stanza. Then after we knew those lines we would learn the next part. We would not hand a learner the 100 number facts and say, "Learn them!" First we would establish meaning so (s)he understands what (s)he is doing as (s)he adds or multiplies, and then (s)he would practice responding quickly to only a few facts. After (s)he learned those, (s)he would practice some additional ones.

While it seems obvious that we should practice a small amount that is meaningful, there are many violations of this principle. In their zeal, teachers often attempt to teach, and students unsuccessfully attempt to learn, too much in one practice period. The result is a braid of confusion with frustration resulting from effort that is unsuccessful. Common examples of misuse of this principle of working on small meaningful amounts are:

a. Working on twenty spelling words in one period.
b. Studying all the number facts that have been missed (assuming that there are more than 3–5).

c. Trying to learn all about _____ (Magellan, the Civil War, the geography of a country) at one time.

d. Trying to learn everything that was missed on a test in one practice period.

The student and/or teacher should select a *small meaningful part* of what is to be learned (the first half of the "five times tables," 2–5 spelling words, what Magellan did to get ready for his voyage, 2–5 things that were missed on the test), learn those things, and then stop. Long practice periods usually are inefficient and often ineffective.

The more able learner can, of course, handle a greater amount (5–6 spelling words rather than 1–2) but (s)he, too, should practice *intensively for a short period of time* and then stop for a while. After a rest (which can be doing something related but not exactly the same as what (s)he just practiced), (s)he may resume practice of what was learned in the previous practice period to see if it is remembered. If it is, some new material can be added. If some things have been forgotten, those should be practiced again for a short time and then the student should stop for a while.

2. How long should each practice period be? The psychological generalization that guides teaching is: *Short, intense highly motivated°* *practice periods produce more learning which is better remembered* than long drawn out periods. Of course, the practice period must be long enough to get something done but not so long that attention and effort wane from fatigue or loss of interest. It is amazing what a few minutes spent on highly motivated practice will produce in a student's learning and remembering. Short intense practice periods several times a day will produce more learning than double that amount of time at one setting.

It is possible to expend too much time on ineffective or unmotivated practice. Common errors are:

a. Writing a spelling word 20 times.

b. Studying number facts for a half hour.

c. Doing 30 examples to develop speed.

d. Doing 25 of the same kind of problem.

e. Going over the same thing for 20 minutes.

°Motivated practice is considered to be practice when the learner is really intending to improve, to "learn it" not just to "do it."

Obviously, the more complex the task, the longer it takes to do it. Practicing the writing of introductory paragraphs will take more time, even if you do only three of them, than the time needed to practice three spelling words. The length of the practice period must be tailored to the kind of task and the maturity of the learner. Highly skilled performers who spend many hours on practice, still practice one thing intensively for short periods.

It is amazing to see how much can be accomplished in five minutes of intense highly motivated practice. For some tasks, 10–20 minutes may be necessary. If more time is needed, often it is better to break the task into parts, each of which is practiced for a short period. Later when each part is learned, a longer period may be needed to put them together.

3. How close together should practice periods be scheduled? The psychological generalization that guides teaching is: *Many practice periods close together should be scheduled at the beginning of learning.* This *massing* of practice results in fast learning. *Once something has been learned, practice periods should be scheduled farther and farther apart.* This *distributing* of practice results in long retention of the material that has been learned. When something new is introduced, there should be several brief practice periods within a short period of time (massing practice). Other practice periods should occur during that day and on subsequent days. Once something has been learned, a review once a week and then once a month (distributing practice) will more nearly ensure remembering. You will recognize these familiar violations of this principle:
   a. Taking a spelling test on Friday with no further attention to those words in subsequent weeks.
   b. Becoming familiar with an episode in history and then moving on, never reviewing or reconsidering that episode.
   c. Learning people's names, and then not thinking of them again so the names are forgotten.
   d. Reading a book or article, never reviewing what it was about, and soon it's forgotten.

Working on smaller amounts of a task in a short practice period encourages massing of practice. For example, if a student is working on four number facts, each of those can be practiced many times (massed) in a one minute practice period. After they are learned, reviewing those facts twice a week, once a week and then once a month (distributed) will more nearly ensure their being remembered.

If a student misses something during a practice period, he should come back to it again and again in a short period of time (massed practice). For example, if he is studying the last half of his 7 times tables and he misses 7 x 8, his practice should be: 7 x 8 =, 7 x 6 =, 7 x 8 =, 7 x 7 =, 7 x 8 =, 7 x 9 =, 7 x 8 = until the answer to 7 x 8 is automatic. At his next practice period he should again check 7 x 8. If he knows it, only occasional repetitions are necessary. He should *not*, however, repeat the same response 7 x 8 =, 7 x 8 =, 7 x 8 = without another fact or two between. Repeating the same fact requires no thinking, just "parroting" which is ineffective for learning. He must always be making a "thinking-intention-of-learning" response.

When practicing reading, it is important to mass practice on *any word missed.* Usually the student should reread the sentence that contains the word that was missed. At the end of the page (s)he should go back to that word and read it again. If it isn't remembered, (s)he should reread the whole sentence for a clue. At the end of the story (s)he should again read any words missed to make sure they are remembered. It is helpful to make a list of missed words with the page number on which each word occurred so the student can mass practice by working on them several times that same day. The next day (s)he should reread them and relearn any that have been forgotten. If a student is missing more than 2–3 words on a page, that book is too hard for reading instruction (too much needs to be learned in one practice period). (S)he should change to a book in which it is possible to learn, each day, the unknown words.

4. How will the student know how well (s)he is doing (knowledge of results)? Practice without feedback that lets the student know that he is right or, if he isn't, what is wrong, is seldom effective. The more immediate the knowledge of results, the easier it is for the student to improve performance or correct errors. Consequently, *the student must have access to knowledge of results,* either from written material or from a person.

In practicing sports, knowing where the ball landed, if the shot hit the target, how much time is being cut down in running, etc., are obvious necessities. Not so obvious, but equally important, is the information that tells the student how well he is doing in classroom practice.

Frequent monitoring of students when they are practicing enables the adult to "spot check" and quickly identify any student who needs help. Monitoring also gives successful students knowledge of results ("That's right," "You're getting them all," "That's coming along well") which in turn increases their motivation to learn.

A test becomes a highly motivated practice period when the student learns, as soon as possible after a test, what was right and, if something was missed, what the answer should have been. Violations of the principle of knowledge of results occur when papers aren't checked or tests aren't returned for several weeks or not at all.

In summary, a great deal of learning time can be saved by introducing all practice with the "3 M's" of *meaning, modeling and monitoring* and then by applying the four principles of effective practice:

1. Practice small meaningful parts and add more only when those are learned.
2. Schedule short intense practice periods where the student is highly motivated to "do it better."
3. Mass practice periods at the beginning so the material is learned quickly. Then distribute practice so it is long remembered.
4. Enable the student to get knowledge of results while (s)he is practicing or as soon as possible afterwards.

After you develop meaning, modeling and monitoring, when you apply these four principles, make sure the learner is doing the practice, not you; that *he* says the answer, *he* writes the words, *he* intends to learn rather than merely watching you do it, or listening to you tell him about it.

As a teacher, your job is to encourage him by *helping him to be right,* letting him know when he *is* right, helping him to realize *when* he has learned, what he has learned, and *what he still needs to practice.* Your support, approval and reinforcement will help him develop more confidence in himself so eventually he can become his own teacher and design his own practice periods—something he will need as an assist to learning throughout his life.

For additional information:

Book:
Hunter, Madeline. *Teach More—Faster!* TIP Publications. P.O. Box 514, El Segundo, California 90245.

Films:

"Teach More—Faster!" Part I, Part II, Part III. black and white. 30 minutes.

"Improving Practice." color. 30 minutes.

"Helping in Reading." color. 30 minutes.

"Helping in Math." color. 30 minutes.

"Effective Practice." black and white. 40 minutes.

SPECIAL PURPOSE FILMS
26740 Latigo Shore Drive
Malibu, California 90265

DO'S AND DON'TS OF EFFECTIVE PRACTICE

1. Do work on short meaningful units.
   "Let's learn these 3 words."
   "Let's concentrate on your 8's."
   "What were the 2 words on this page that slowed you down?"

1. Don't work on a long unrelated series.
   "Let's work on all 10 of these words."
   "Let's work on the 100 multiplication facts."
   "Let's work on all the new words in this story."

2. Do work for short concentrated periods.
   "Let's see how much you can get done in the next 5 minutes."
   "Let's see how many you can learn before recess."

2. Don't drag out practice periods.
   "Let's see how much you can learn by tomorrow."
   "I'll be here all morning to help you with your math."

3. Do review something a student learned when you previously worked with him.
   "Let's see if you remember your 8's."
   "Let's check the words you learned last time and then move on."

3. Don't skip an opportunity to review previously learned material.
   "You learned your 8's last week, let's move on to your 9's."
   "You learned 5 words yesterday, let's try 5 new words."

4. Do practice something new in many different contexts.
   "What two numbers will make 5? What other two numbers will make 5? What other two numbers, etc.?"
   "Use 'courageous' in a sentence that will help us know what it means. Can you think of another sentence? Use it in a still different sentence."

4. Don't practice something new only once.
   "What two numbers make 5? What two numbers make 6? What two numbers make 7?"
   "Use 'courageous' in a sentence. Use 'novel' in a sentence. Use 'mystery' in a sentence."

5. Do have a student practice something new several times while you are there.

"Now that you know that word, I will come back to see if you remember it in a few minutes."

"Tell me your new word before you go out for recess."

"Remember the word you told me just before recess, what was it? Good, I'll ask you again just before I leave."

6. Do give a student knowledge of results. "I'll nod my head each time you get it right. If I don't nod, you need to think again."

"As soon as you finish the first row, I'll check it and let you know how you've done."

"I'll go over your paper at noon so you can see how much you've learned."

5. Don't have a student learn something new and then not check to see that he remembers it.

"You learned a new word, be sure you remember it."

"Now that you've finished, we won't work on that anymore."

6. Don't leave a student wondering how he did.

"A check on your paper means I've seen it."

"I'll return these papers after vacation."

"Just keep on practicing, it will be good for you."

MAKING MISTAKES PRODUCTIVE

A mistake productive? How could that be? A mistake is objective evidence that a student "doesn't know" or "can't do." As such, it alerts us to the fact that something needs to be learned. Without that mistake, the learner's problem might go undetected and therefore unremediated with the resultant possibility of more serious problems later on. A mistake uncorrected is the same as a mistake undetected, both could eventually swamp a learner. A productive mistake is one which is corrected and the right response learned thereby leaving the student stronger, with more confidence in his own ability and more ego strength to support him in the future mistakes which are inevitable.

When a learner makes a mistake there are two things he doesn't know. He doesn't know the answer to the question that was asked and he doesn't know the question to which his incorrect answer really belongs. Thus, if he says 5 x 8 = 45 he doesn't know the answer to 5 x 8 and he doesn't know the combination to which 45 is the right answer. In the same way if he says Lincoln was our first president, he doesn't know the name of our first president and he also doesn't know when Lincoln was president.

Both errors must be corrected. He has learned only half of what he needs to know when he learns that 5 x 8 = 40 or that Washington was our first president. Then he has corrected half of his error. He also needs to learn that 45 is the answer to 5 x 9 and when Lincoln was president.

There are three steps to dealing productively with mistakes.

1. *Supplying the question to which the answer belongs.* Usually, the teacher supplies, in a way that is not demeaning, the question to which his answer belongs. "Forty-five would be the right answer if I had asked about 5 x 9. Now what would 5 x 8 be?" Supplying the question to which the incorrect answer belongs not only gives needed information to the learner but maintains his dignity, feelings of worth and demonstrates he had important information, he just got it in the wrong place. To say, "You're wrong," or "That's not correct" makes even the most resilient learner feel embarrassed or foolish and unless that result is the teacher's intent, such negative feelings should be avoided.

2. *Supplying prompts.* Prompts are questions or suggestions that point the learner toward the right answer. When they are needed the teacher supplies prompts to help the student locate or figure out

68

the answer. "If you bought eight nickel candy bars how much would you spend?" or "If you bought five nickel candy bars how much would that be? Six? Seven? Now eight? then how much is 5 x 8?" To prompt him on the first president the teacher might say, "Our national capital is named after him," or "His name begins with W."

3. *Checking to see if learning has occurred.* The teacher should return to that question before too much time has passed to check whether the student has learned and remembered the corrections to *both* of his errors. "Now what is the answer to 5 x 8? And how much are 5 x 9? Good, now you know both of them!"

When a learner knows he is responsible for correcting his error and he will be checked as to whether or not he has remembered the answer, he is much more motivated to learn the correct response. Often the teacher can trigger his intent by, "I'll come back to you in a minute and then you'll get it just right."

Let's follow these three steps to correcting errors in our example of knowing the first president. The teacher might say, "Lincoln was certainly one of our most important presidents, but his term of office was during the Civil War." (Supplying the question to which his answer belongs) "Will it help if I tell you our first president's name began with W?" (Prompts to help him generate the right answer) If the student still doesn't know, the teacher or another student supplies the correct answer. There is no point in a student merely guessing when he doesn't have the information. *The teacher must then check to make sure the learner has heard the correct information.* "Now, what would you write in answer to the question, who was our first president? Good, now you know it."

We cannot assume that just because something has been said, it has been heard. Also students quickly learn that you are going to check so they listen more carefully with an intent to remember. As one student remarked, "If you miss something in Miss Brown's class, she gives you a chance to learn it and you'd better listen 'cause, sure as heck, she'll ask you again before the end of the period!" (Checking to see if it has been learned and remembered)

Let's look at a third example. A student has written "dessert" when he means "desert." The teacher might say, (1) "You wrote the word that means something good that you eat at the end of a meal, dessert." (Giving the question to which his answer belongs. (2) "Do you know how to spell the word that means a hot, dry sandy land? What letter could you leave out and still have all the letter sounds you need?" (Prompts) (3) "Good, now whenever you spell it with two "S's," what will you mean? If you use just one "S" what will that word mean? I'll ask you again at the end of the period so you'll be sure to remember it from now on." (Checking to see if he remembers)

In summary, students' mistakes are important signals that alert us to the fact that something is wrong. A mistake is destructive only if it remains uncorrected or results in a student losing confidence in himself as a learner. A mistake corrected by a teacher who is following these three principles can be an important assist to learning, both in terms of the elimination of misunderstood or unknown material, and in terms of the student's increased confidence in himself as a learner when he corrects that mistake.

CHANGING WAITING TIME
TO LEARNING TIME

MEETING PLAN

Long Range Objectives
Teachers will develop facility and artistry in the use of "sponge" activities to encourage highly motivated practice and/or anticipatory set.

Staff Meeting Objective
Teachers will identify and discuss strategies to increase students' learning through utilization of sponge activities during "waiting time."

Preparation for Staff Meeting
Prior to the meeting, staff members should have the opportunity to read "Waiting Time Becomes Learning Time" on page 75. If that is not possible, the principal or a staff member should assume the responsibility for presenting the content to the staff.

Staff Discussion
The major part of the staff meeting should be spent in small groups (3-5 staff members, clusters of grade levels, not single grade levels as that encourages narrow thinking) addressing themselves to the following questions:
1. In which academic areas do our students need practice?
2. What short activities would give them the needed practice?
3. How can the practice be made meaningful and stimulating?
4. How will we identify those for whom it is appropriate and those for whom it is not?
5. How can we build different degrees of difficulty into the same practice so each student will find a "catch hold" place that is right for him?

71

6. What can we do to build in the necessary learning steps so those who can't, soon can?

To avoid merely "talking about problems" rather than resolving them, each group should present to the total group some sponge activities they have designed. A better product will be achieved if the discussion groups start one week and continue to the following week, giving teachers two staff sessions plus a week of "try out" in the classrooms before they present conclusions (and techniques) to the total staff.

For most efficient utilization, sponge activities should be categorized according to content (Math—number facts, word problems, etc.; Reading—sight vocabulary, initial consonants, etc.; Vocabulary development—word meaning, synonyms, etc.). Sponge activities should be recorded in some form so each teacher's good ideas are available to other staff members. The resultant list of sponge activities can be duplicated and distributed to each staff member.

It is also professionally productive for the staff to take one strand, such as counting, vocabulary development, or word problems and develop a continuum of activities which increase in difficulty from those appropriate for very young children to activities appropriate for gifted older children. Don't make the mistake of assigning grade levels to different activities, instead focus on levels of increasing difficulty so the teacher begins where the students are and takes them on from there. The following is a sample of ascending difficulty: "Make up a word problem using these numerals and this operation. Be sure your problem has a question that makes us perform the operation."

a.	$2+3=$	i.	$105 \div 5=$	q.	$2/3 \times 1/3=$
b.	$7-5=$	j.	$750 \div 25=$	r.	$2/3 \div 1/2=$
c.	$23+29=$	k.	$1/2+1/2=$	s.	$.50+.25=$
d.	$108-49=$	l.	$1/2+3/4=$	t.	$1.37-.25=$
e.	$3 \times 9=$	m.	$3/4-1/4=$	u.	$.25 \times 2=$
f.	$5 \times 16=$	n.	$3/4-2/3=$	v.	$.25 \times .75=$
g.	$27 \times 45=$	o.	$1-3/4-1/3=$	w.	$2 \div .25=$
h.	$10 \div 2=$	p.	$2/3 \times 5=$	x.	$.75 \div 5=$

(you add y and z)

If your staff is like most, they will find that not only students have difficulty assigning meaning to many of the operations, they are mechanically performing, so do some of their teachers. Staff members also experience the "So that's what we're doing!" insight that makes the math program of your school not only more meaningful, but much better taught and longer remembered. Quite a dividend from a staff meeting!

The staff may wish to separate into sub groups, according to their special aptitudes and interest, and work out many such sequences to share with the total group.

Follow-up

As a follow-up to these meetings, the principal and staff members should take the opportunity to observe in different classrooms to see each other's use of sponge activities. This observation is possible when teachers train their students to independently start their own work or independently engage in sponge activities as soon as they enter the classroom, thereby freeing their teacher to "look in next door."

If the staff wishes to extend their professional skills even further, the principal and staff should devote some staff meeting time and visiting time to investigate the three other ways that class time is dissipated, with no learning return, which are listed on page 75. First in his/her own classroom, and then by visiting in other classrooms, teachers should observe to determine:

1. Are some students working on assignments that are too difficult for them? Are some working on assignments where they are successful without really trying? Spelling assignments will reveal surprising examples as students who never get all the words right and those who always do are identified. Teachers might also look at the remedial and accelerated readers who are working in the same social studies book.
2. Is what the student is doing in order to learn as efficient as it should be? Are there too many of the same kind of examples or is the opposite problem evident, only one example of each kind, so there is no opportunity for the student to perceive improvement from one example to the next one that requires the same skills?

Are students wasting time copying the questions when they should focus their energy on developing better answers? Are they getting all the problems copied and then doing only half of them rather than solving each problem as they go?

73

3. Can you defend what the student is learning as being useful and important rather than justifying it because it has "always been taught?" A good criterion is to determine how many times you have used that particular skill recently. If you haven't needed it, it's highly likely the student won't use it. You have used the skill of reading in this book and applying that information to solve some problems in your daily life. Now there's an important assignment for students. How can they apply what they are currently learning in their everyday life?

Principal's Responsibility

The principal should also model sponge activities in assemblies and student gatherings as well as while teachers are gathering for staff meetings, in parent meetings and district meetings. Even though those groups do not need to practice a skill, they surely will benefit from an appropriate anticipatory set. (What question are we trying to answer by this meeting? Be ready to list the topics we should consider today. Determine the primary factors that are interfering with (contributing to) . . . .)

It is productive for the principal to take a teacher's class for a short period and free that teacher to visit other classrooms in the school. The anxiety of the principal and the staff may go up a little by such visiting but the professional skills of the principal and staff members are guaranteed to go up a whole lot more! As the principal observes in classes (s)he should be noting the answers to questions listed on page 75 to stimulate discussion with individual teachers and as valid content for future staff meetings.

Dividends

As staff members develop creativity, efficiency and effectiveness in the use of sponge activities, students should become better focused, practice more effectively, need less practice and achieve more learning. In addition, there will be the surprising dividend of a marked reduction in discipline problems which occur during transitions and at the beginning and end of lessons.

The most important dividend will be realized as teachers share ideas and techniques and by visiting each other become more sophisticated and creative in program development for the whole school.

WAITING TIME BECOMES LEARNING TIME

Classrooms have been accused of being slaughterhouses of time. Time is killed, and much of it wasted in the same way that, in the past, animals were slaughtered and much of them wasted. Now, industry with its emphasis on extracting everything of value, has eliminated such waste and "everything but the moo" is used.

In education, the current emphasis on accountability has forced similar conservation of our most valuable educational resource—the time and energy of teacher and learner. In classrooms, that precious time and energy can be expended with great learning dividends or dissipated with little or no learning return. Educational "conservation" can minimize or eliminate waste that occurs:

1. *When time and energy are devoted to a learning objective that is so difficult it is unattainable within a reasonable time, or to an objective that already has been attained.* Waste of time and energy occur when a student tries valiantly but unsuccessfully to accomplish a learning task which he never should have been assigned in the first place. Asking a remedial reader to read the social studies book or to solve word problems in math which require reading at his grade level, constitutes such a wasteful teaching error. Equally serious is the dissipation of a student's time and energy on something that is too easy or so well learned it needs no additional practice.

2. *When time and energy are expended inefficiently and ineffectively while supposedly directed to learning.* Classic examples of this waste are: "Write it twenty times"; lessons where only one learner is responding while the rest, supposedly listening, in reality have their minds out of gear; students working on something longer than is productive, such as doing 50 examples of the same type.

3. *When time and energy are devoted to an objective that is not important or worth the effort.* Memorizing endless lists of names and dates, capitals and states, copying and recopying, answering unimportant questions, and perfecting trivial tasks are classroom examples that occur too frequently.

4. *When valuable student time is expended in WAITING, WAITING, WAITING!* Serious erosion of time and energy occurs when learners are waiting; waiting for the class to start, waiting for the reading group to gather, waiting for papers to be passed out

or collected, waiting to be dismissed, waiting for the teacher to get to them. All this waiting leaves students with nothing to do but to entertain themselves. Usually they fill this time by daydreaming, talking and playing with their friends, or getting into trouble.

Regardless of whether students sop up waiting time with productive or nonproductive activities, additional valuable time is lost as the teacher has to get students' attention and refocus them for the next learning.

While all four of these sources of waste result in serious dissipation of time and energy, professional competence can eliminate most of the time lost by the first three. Consequently, this chapter will be addressed to the productive utilization of time which unavoidably must be devoted to waiting. To accomplish this economy, the technique of using "sponge" activities to productively utilize rather than dissipate waiting time has been developed at the laboratory school of UCLA. These activities can be modified or tailored for use in any classroom, at any age level, with any content, for any students.

"Sponge activities" is the name of learning opportunities which "sop up" those precious droplets of "waiting time" which otherwise would be lost. Sponge activities are designed to:

1. Review or extend previous learnings.
2. Build readiness or "set" for the learning which is about to occur.
3. Eliminate the discipline problems which can be generated in transition periods.

Sponge activities, because they occur during transitions or at the beginning and end of an assignment, must be designed to accommodate late arrivals (latecomers can join in the activity without feeling lost) or early departures (students can be dismissed or depart without missing something essential). Whenever there is an unavoidable waiting period before a planned activity can start, or when students finish an assignment and have some time left over, the effective teacher utilizes this time either to strengthen learnings that need extension and/or additional practice, or to prepare learners to move more successfully into the next learning. New or unfamiliar material should not be introduced in sponge periods.

Sponge Activities That Provide Additional Practice
Or Extend Previous Learning

The following examples of sponge activities are designed to give additional practice or extend a previous learning. These practice periods conform to research that suggests that several short, intense practice periods usually are more effective than one long period.

Mathematics

These examples should trigger the countless possibilities appropriate for a particular classroom:

1. As a group is gathering (coming into the room or coming to small group instruction), students can practice counting by 1's, 2's, 5's, 10's, 3's, etc. The difficulty is determined by students' practice needs. Counting may be done in unison so those who are not facile get continual prompting, or every student can *think* of the next number in the series, and then any student to whom the teacher points must say the next number. The difficulty of the practice can vary from counting to 10 forward and/or backward, to extremely complex patterns. Latecomers who join the group can, by listening, know what is going on. Simple or complex counting is an equally effective sponge activity for dismissal. The student giving the correct answer leaves, while the rest who need additional practice continue to focus on the next response. A teacher can individualize by deliberately selecting easy or difficult examples so certain students are sometimes excused first, sometimes last, as they respond to the example appropriate to their practice needs.

2. The teacher can model verbal word problems utilizing social studies content ("If Columbus sailed five weeks, etc."), or focus on real life episodes at school ("It took us 15 minutes to finish, etc."), or use the names of learners in the group ("Paul made three home runs, etc."). Solving or generating word problems gives excellent practice in application of the already learned math operations to many different life situations. Having students make up a word problem that will fit a number problem which the teacher puts on the chalkboard ($10 + 2$ or $250 \div 5$) enables learners to test, practice and refine their mathematical understanding. Incidentally, such practice can dramatically reveal any lack of ability to apply what has been learned to real life situations, thereby alerting the teacher to needed instruction.

3. Number facts or short, mental computations ($3 + 5 + 6 + 1 =$) give practice and develop agility in computing without paper and pencil. Combinations must be short enough, however, so new

problems are constantly available to learners who join the group. Problems can be made as easy or as difficult as is appropriate for individual members of the group, and each learner can respond to a problem at the degree of difficulty appropriate for him. This type of practice also can be used for dismissal.

Language

These suggestions are designed to trigger the creativity of each teacher to meet the practice needs of his/her class.

1. "Hangman" is a game that can be led by teacher or child. A short line is placed on the chalkboard to represent each letter of the word the leader has in mind. The group guesses letters. If they are correct, the letter is placed on the appropriate line. If the letter is not in the word, it is recorded on the chalkboard, and a part of the body of the man to be hung is drawn (head, neck, arms, etc.). The object is to guess the word before the man is completed, or "hung." The teacher can use this game to review reading and spelling words, important names and concepts, or it can also be used to introduce the lesson that immediately follows. An example of the latter might be, "This is a word that describes my favorite food (or best friend)," which acts as a precursor to a lesson where the objective is the use of vivid, descriptive words. An excellent use of this game is for the first student in the room in the morning (or the beginning of the period after recess), to start the game so each student as he enters can join in by looking at the letters that have been used and subtracting them from those still remaining in the alphabet. This sponge activity gives the teacher time to take roll, get things ready, etc., while the students are responsible for productively engaging themselves in a learning activity.

2. Sponge activities that give practice in phonics can be as simple as, "I spy with my little eye something that begins (ends) with B," or as complex as, "Something that begins with *BL* and ends with *D*." Rhyming words, middle sounds, words with silent letters, etc., can be practiced effectively in these "tag ends" of time.

3. For alphabet practice, "What letter comes after/before *M*?" "Which would come first in the dictionary, *blue* or *black*?" "Let's think of words that start with these two letters," are a few exam-

ples of the countless activities which a creative teacher might generate.

4. Synonymes, homonymes, and vocabulary development lend themselves to sponge activities. "Let's think of all the words that mean shades of red." "How can you use the sound of red to mean two different things?" (The color was red. I read the book.) "What are some other words that mean brave?" These are a few of the limitless activities that contribute significantly to vocabulary development of the productive use of scraps of time.

Other Content Areas

The stampedes of turning in work at dismissals can be eliminated by sponge activities. "When I take your paper, be ready to tell me one thing you learned today in social studies," requires motivated recall which is an excellent type of practice. "Those people who are wearing plaid (blue, oxfords, a repeated pattern, etc.) may go," requires practice in discrimination. The difficulty of the content may be varied from recognition of colors to complex discriminations, generating alternatives or divergent thinking (two colors that are opposite on the color wheel, different ways you could _____, and an unusual use for _____). Again, it needs to be emphasized that in sponge activities learnings or ways of thinking must be familiar, responses which need practice for fluency or extension. *New content should not be introduced.* "What is the noun phrase of this sentence?" is appropriate only if students know what a noun phrase is and need practice in identifying one in a variety of contexts.

These are but a few examples from a universe of sponge activities, developed by the creative teacher, which give students needed practice that is interesting and effective. The essential ingredient is the identification of a skill, concept, discrimination, etc., which has been learned but which should be strengthened or extended by additional highly motivated short practice periods. The essential guideline is that a late arrival would quickly recognize what is to be done and join in, and an early departure would not miss something essential.

In work periods, the time between the first and last student who finishes can be utilized effectively by a sponge activity which extends the learning of the assignment just completed. Examples of extending sponge activities in language might be: "If you finish early,

a. write the question you would have asked to check understanding of the story."

b. write a different ending."
c. list the parts you liked best."
d. make a picture about the story with only one thing that is different from the story."
e. write what the main character might say/do/think if he came to our classroom."

If the assignment is math:

f. "Make up a word problem to go with the first number problem."
g. "Make up some problems where you regroup only from the tens to the ones (or from the hundreds to the tens")."
h. "Make up some division problems where there are remainders."

Sponge activities which are provided for the end of assignment can extend students' learnings into more complex application and eliminate the "What do I do now?" problem.

Sponge Activities To Create Set

Another important use of sponge activities is based on the psychological principle of *mental set*, or predisposition to perform. All teachers have experienced the frustrating phenomenon of intellectual inertia at the beginning of a lesson or work period which erodes initial participation. ("Oh, is *that* what we're supposed to do?") Skillful teachers have learned to devote time to develop focus of students, elicit their interest, "shift their minds into gear," and increase their motivation to learn. Often this can be accomplished by a sponge activity while the group is gathering. A question on the chalkboard is one way of developing learner focus while he is waiting for his group to gather. "How was Daniel Boone like an astronaut?" can start thinking for the discussion that immediately follows. "Read the first page of the story and think of a question to ask your friends," starts a reading group. "What question stumped our group yesterday?" focuses attention on today's search. "Be ready to tell the two problems Bill had," reviews yesterday's discussion and gets minds in gear for today's follow-up.

To design a sponge activity that will promote motivation and set to perform, a teacher needs to examine the ensuing lesson and decide what students should be thinking about or considering beforehand that will provide a springboard for the new learning. This "prior propulsion" not only focuses the learner, but provides impetus that will carry a lesson much farther with efficiency and effectiveness. In addition to focusing potential, sponge activities also contribute to students' assuming

80

responsibility for starting themselves and, if the question is written on the board, for practicing reading and generating responses.

The following examples are springboards for the creative teacher to develop appropriate activities for his/her own group.

1. "Be ready to describe the main character in two sentences."
2. "Think of three smells you like."
3. "Which explorer would you like to be? Why?"
4. "Make up a word problem using multiplication or division. Be ready to tell it to the group."
5. "Make up one sentence using these words . . . ."
6. "How would you solve this problem?"
7. After an input designed to stimulate creative expression, learners can be asked to, "Signal when you have thought of the sentence you will use to begin your story (or poem)," or "the color and shape you will paint first," or "the first thing you need to do." By using this technique, learners are dismissed when they are ready to begin work rather than having them go to their seats, chew their pencils and hope for inspiration.

At the end of a lesson the same kinds of questions constitute an excellent review and contribute to practice in summarizing or extracting the essence of an activity before being excused from a group. For example:

1. "What new words did we learn today?"
2. "What did we do that you liked?"
3. "What do you think were the most important points?"
4. "What part of the story did you enjoy?"
5. "What is the next thing you will do?"

Use Sponge Activities Daily During "Waiting Time"

Teachers who systematically make use of sponge activities which are appropriate to their group in order to give students practice or create an anticipatory mental set will find their students arrive more promptly because there is something interesting to do and are more alert because they are used to "turning on" thinking as soon as they arrive. As a result, many discipline problems will be eliminated, and valuable time which otherwise would be wasted is utilized. By using sponge activities, "waiting time" becomes a powerful "learning time" which teachers and children enjoy and which pays tremendous dividends in increased achievement.

TEACHING TO ACHIEVE
INDEPENDENT LEARNERS

MEETING PLAN

Long Range Objective
Learners will increase the time that they are productively engaged in learning tasks without direct supervision or assistance from the teacher.

Staff Meeting Objectives
Teachers will discuss steps in teaching for independence in learners.

Teachers will develop examples of independent activities.

Teachers will implement plans to achieve independent learning in their classrooms.

Preparation for Staff Meeting
Teachers should have the opportunity to read the section "Teaching for Independence" on page 85 before the meeting. If that is not possible, the principal or a staff member should present the information contained in the article. An outline on the chalkboard or distributing a short (1-2 page) summary is helpful as a reference for use during the meeting. It is suggested that this meeting be subsequent to the meeting on Improving Students' Behavior as reinforcement techniques are essential to achieving independent learners.

Staff Discussion
The discussion should emphasize:

1. Independence in learning is not achieved by edict, admonition, or experience alone. Independence is most predictably achieved when it is taught.
2. The skill of working independently is acquired gradually, not all at once. It *is* all right to begin teaching independence with easy tasks or games that involve no special academic learning in order that students practice functioning by themselves without problems.

It is *not* all right to continue with only games and busywork once students have learned to work without needing teacher assistance. Then students are ready to practice academic material or learn new material independently.

3. Eventually, independent activities should be used to strengthen, extend or enrich learning. Material that is completely new to the individual is usually learned most effectively when there is teacher guidance. The psychological principle that supports this statement is: *maximum guidance at initial stages of learning not only will accelerate learning but will minimize errors which later must be corrected.* After initial stages of learning, teacher guidance should be withdrawn gradually so the learner assumes increasing responsibility for developing the fluency, accuracy and speed of his/her own performance.

4. There should be opportunities for students to engage in independent creative activity, pursuing their own interests and inclinations as soon as they have learned the skills to do so productively.

After staff discussion, when teachers are familiar with the purpose of independent activities and can identify the difference between Type I, II, III, activities, the staff should divide into small discussion groups whose members are from at least two grade levels. The task of the small groups is to develop examples of Type I, II, III activities that would be appropriate for the children they teach. Even though there are several teachers at one grade level, for greatest productivity, discussion groups should have members from adjoining grades such as K-1-2 or 1-2 or 3-4-5 or 5-6. Regardless of the grade or class composition, some students will require simpler Type I tasks if they are to become independent. Other students will be ready for much more complex tasks and need that challenge if they are not to become bored or "time-wasters."

From these small discussion groups should come lists of possible activities of all three types. This list can be duplicated for use (with extension and modification for different abilities and age levels) by the entire staff.

Follow-up
Following the staff meeting, each teacher should schedule a period of Type I activities in order to diagnose his/her class and make a list of those students who can work productively and independently at Type I activities. These students then should have opportunities to work

with Type II and III independent activities. The list also should identify those students who cannot sustain themselves at Type I activities and those who cannot even get started. Special learning opportunities suggested on page 87 must be provided so these students begin to develop the ability to work by themselves. A copy of each teacher's diagnostic student list should be available to the principal so he can add his/her knowledge and effort to the progress of students toward independence.

At the end of a month of staff effort directed to teaching for independence, most students should be able to work independently for 20-30 minutes. Some still may be on Type I activities. Most students will be on Type II or III, but teacher judgements must continually be made in terms of each learner's actual classroom performance.

The Principal's Responsibilities

It is the task of the principal to monitor, encourage and reinforce the development of independent learners in each classroom as well as to alert parents to the staff effort being directed to this objective which is so necessary to students throughout life. The principal also needs to provide opportunities for teachers to visit each other's classrooms to promote exchange of successful practice and to stimulate creative effort.

Dividends

No matter whether the staff is traditional or innovative, or the school is graded or non graded, self-contained or team taught, open or traditional, teaching for independent learning is guaranteed to produce constantly accelerating dividends in student learning and teacher satisfaction.

TEACHING TO ACHIEVE
INDEPENDENT LEARNERS *

The learner who is in charge of himself, who can make choices and pursue his interests, who can continue his learning without constant assistance and/or supervision by the teacher, is likely to become a self-propelling, lifelong learner. Such a learner is our paramount goal in education today. Most students, in the past, have not achieved this goal to a sufficient degree.

Many of our new organizational schemes, open education, team teaching, nongrading, and individualized instruction are focused on the goal of independence and self-propulsion in learning. Organizational schemes, however, only create an environment in which this goal can be achieved. The organizational plan in no way insures that the goal of independence *will* be a predictable product. Only skillful teaching can accomplish that.

If learners are to become independent, teachers must assume responsibility for teaching the behavior of "learning independently," in the same way that they assume responsibility for teaching "reading" in order that learners become literate. Some students, of course, learn to read and learn to work independently with little or no instruction. The majority of learners, however, will more predictably achieve these goals with the professional assistance a teacher is trained to give.

Let's look at some reasons why the objective: "The learner works independently and productively on self-selected or assigned activities," is a goal worthy of major teaching effort. In this objective, "independently" means with minimal teacher supervision and assistance, "productively" means with learning gain for himself and no disturbance to others, "self-selected activities" are those he chooses from available alternatives and "assigned" are those activities determined by the teacher.

Advantages to the Learner:

1. (S)he has asssistance with and practice in selecting from alternatives thereby become a decision maker—a skill (s)he will need throughout his life.
2. (S)he has the practice necessary to develop facility in determining what to do, following directions and completing assignments without help.

---

*This article was prepared in collaboration with Dr. Dorothy Lloyd, Graduate School of Education, University of California, Los Angeles.

3. Support, success or remediation can constantly be built into his/her decision making, so (s)he will productively meet rather than retreat from future decisions.
4. (S)he receives direct feedback from the real world as to the state of his/her independence.
5. (S)he can direct his/her practice in order to develop new learnings and reinforce old ones, thereby testing, strengthening and improving his/her own learning strategies.
6. (S)he has the opportunity to develop skills in working with other students as a member of an independent learning group.
7. (S)he becomes responsible for the acquisition, use, care and storage of materials.

These seven dividends in themselves would make teaching for independence a worthy objective. Additional dividends accrue to the teacher.

Advantages to the Teacher:

1. As (s)he circulates throughout the class and observes learners in independent activities, a teacher secures important information about those learners that is available in no other way.
2. Learning is no longer completely dependent on the teacher's availability but can occur without his/her direct supervision.
3. The teacher becomes available to work *undisturbed* with small groups or individual learners.
4. The teacher has the satisfaction of knowing that the self-direction students are developing will be useful throughout their lives.

For a student to become an independent learner, certain supporting behaviors and skills must be achieved. A teacher's edict, admonition, or mere provision of opportunities for independence will not predictably produce the desired behavior. The supporting objectives or component behaviors which must be acquired by the learner if (s)he is to be self-sufficient are:

1. (S)he has demonstrated that (s)he possesses the skills necessary to accomplish the work demanded by the particular independent activity.
2. (S)he can make an appropriate choice from alternatives.
3. (s)he can provide him/herself with the materials needed.
4. (S)he can select and move to an appropriate working space without disturbing others.

5. (S)he can focus on an activity for the time necessary and complete his/her task to an appropriate degree.
6. (S)he can ignore distractors or return to the task after a distraction.
7. (S)he can move from one choice to another without problems.
8. (S)he can return materials to the appropriate place and clean up the space (s)he has occupied.

A learner does not need to have accomplished all these supporting learnings before (s)he engages in independent activity or makes choices. Each of these skills can become the specific teaching objective during the period the student is practicing working without direct supervision. In fact, *most of these skills can be learned only by such guided, monitored and reinforced practice.*

Three different types of independent activities must be considered in order to provide the practice that will extend a student's ability to complete assignments, make choices, and become an increasingly independent learner. The type of activity indicates the complexity of behavior being demanded of the learner. In some classrooms it may be necessary to provide activities at all three levels. In other classrooms, one or two levels may be sufficient.

Type I Activities

The main objective of these activities is to *practice the process of working without direct supervision.* Type I activities are enjoyable, satisfying, easily completed and those for which success is highly probable because the necessary skills have already been learned. While there is no new academic learning involved and many of these activities could be considered "play," it is important to remember that the foundation of independence is the ability to engage oneself in an activity without adult help or supervision. That ability is being learned, practiced, monitored and reinforced by Type I activities.

Examples (for students ages 3-13, additional degrees of complexity would be added for older learners):

Tinker toys, modeling clay, coloring and painting, collage, listening to stories or music at a listening center, individual chalkboards, library books, puzzles, checkers, chess, tic-tac-toe, bingo and any other quiet games for individuals or small groups which the students already know how to play.

Type II Activities:

These are activites that *give needed practice in already learned academic skills.* The objective is to increase the learner's ability to work independently plus increase his speed and/or fluency in school work.

Examples: (Simpler activities are listed, as those for older or more competent children are easier for teachers to generate.)

Math: Activities which require the appropriate level of addition, subtraction, multiplication and division such as bingo, flash cards, magic squares, dittos of missing number patterns, simple job cards or task cards, etc.

Reading-Language: Wordo (bingo word recognition), Quizmo (bingo consonants, blends), scrabble, library books, listening center (following story, phonics), writing practice (letters, words, sentences, paragraphs), story writing, sentence copying or completing with illustration, cut and paste (sequence, letter sounds), plus many commercial activities and teacher made games.

Type III Activities

These are activities that 1) encourage creativity and new learning, 2) practice and/or extend into great complexity learning that is directly related to a current assignment or the student's interest and 3) give students extensive experience in directing their own learning. Activities of this type focus on higher cognitive skills such as analyzing, synthesizing and evaluation. These independent activities may follow a teacher directed lesson, be in lieu of such a lesson or be student generated. They are designed to accomplish high level academic or affective objectives. The ability to work independently has already been achieved through Type I and II activities and that process is merely the vehicle for extended self-direction and achievement in Type III activities.

Examples: A student at this level follows complex oral or written directions to initiate or complete an assignment; writes answers to difficult questions, writes questions to be answered by others, uses learned skills to generate different endings, main ideas, summaries, creative compositions or poetry; solves or creates written word problems; reads a library book for characterizations, comparisons, plot, etc.; uses prepared material to increase specified skills; initiates and/or engages in investigation, experimentation and research projects; works with groups to initiate, develop and test creative ideas.

Teaching to Independence

Now let us take the target objective of independence, the component supporting skills that are necessary to its achievement, the Types of Activities that are stepping stones to its accomplishment and combine them into teaching plans and strategies that will lead to their realization by the students.

Beginning Stages of Independence:

Unless the learners are bringing skills of independence with them, a teacher must start with assignments and choices that enable learners to do something they already know and enjoy. Consequently, the teacher can begin by:

1. Setting up 3–6 activities of Type I which the students may choose.
2. Describing to students what the choices are, where they are located and how many students may participate in each.
3. Giving directions for a) selecting a choice, b) cleaning up when finished, and if appropriate, c) making another choice.
4. Asking students to decide on the activity they will choose.
5. Having a few students model going to, or getting the activity of their choice and beginning.
6. Dismissing the rest of the students, a few at a time, to make choices.
7. Circulating during a 15–20 minute period to diagnose students; their needs, interests, ability to focus and sustain effort. The teacher should make a list of students who need help and what component of independence they lack, as well as reinforce students who demonstrate productive behaviors such as gathering needed materials, focusing on a task, moving from one activity to the next, cleaning up, etc.
8. Giving a signal that will indicate there are 2–3 minutes before clean up.
9. Giving a signal to stop, clean up and return to a designated area for evaluation of their performance in working independently, reinforcing those who respond productively to the signal.

If the first day does not go well, the same procedure should be repeated the next day. If all goes well on the first day, the teacher can introduce a new activity of Type II such as Quizmo (phonics Bingo or scrabble). The whole class should be taught to play it in order to learn the rules and necessary skills. Then this new activity will be added to the choices.

Within the next few days another new activity can be added. Depending on the ability of the learners, the task could vary from copying a sentence selected from four models to writing riddles or stories to go with selected pictures.

Gradually, as students gain proficiency in working independently and

89

develop the necessary skills for making new choices, the teacher will drop some Type I activities and increase Type II activities.

After several days of monitoring the independent activities and finding they are going well, the teacher can work with a small instructional group for a *short* time on a practice or review lesson so (s)he can direct the small group while observing the rest of the class. After the small group, (s)he will need to circulate again among the independent workers to reinforce their productive behaviors. Gradually, the teacher will be able to work with several instructional groups while the other students are productively and independently engaged and, as they finish one task, move to another assignment or activity of their choice.

To avoid boredom, extend learning and continue building skills of independence, new Type II or III activities should be taught and added to the choices each week or so. As new possibilities are added, old activities should be removed so students do not lose interest in them or have a bewilderingly large assortment from which they must choose.

Some students will need special teacher assistance to sustain their effort or even start on independent activities. These learners will constitute one of the first small groups that the teacher works with while (s)he is monitoring the others. The teacher should help those few get started, then leave them for only a few minutes while circulating around the rest of the class. Then (s)he will return to her small "non independent" group reinforcing those who continued to work during teacher absence ("You got a lot done," "You can work well without a teacher"—whatever is appropriate to the task and the maturity of the learner.) The teacher will need to refocus and restart those who didn't sustain themselves. ("Show me what you will do next. "That's right. Now go ahead and I'll be back in a minute to see how you're doing.") Almost all students will eventually respond to this type of remediation which is *teaching* instead of admonishing.

More Advanced Stages of Independence:

When learners are able to work independently, the teacher will provide only Type II and III choices, including creative contracts and assigned job cards. At times, learners should have no assignments, but be completely responsible for scheduling their time productively. Complex games should be available part of the time so a student can develop his/her gaming strategies and work productively with a friend.

In summary, the teacher must thoughtfully consider answers to the following questions and then implement those answers in daily

90

classroom experiences in order to teach learners to function independently:

1. Content—What skills in language, math, reading, social studies, etc., have the students learned well enough to practice indepen- dently? What components of more advanced skills does each learner need to master?
2. Organization—Will the student engage in these activities at his/her usual place or in different areas of the room? Will (s)he work alone or is (s)he ready to work productively with 2–3 others? How many activities should be available each day, at what levels of difficulty? Which one should be changed? How can material be stored and organized so it is easily accessible to students?
3. Records—What kinds of records will be kept so students choices can be monitored? Who will keep this record? Eventually, students should keep their own records, but this too is a learned skill and so must be taught. Above all, avoid a time consuming bookkeeping system that drains a teacher's energy and erodes teaching and learning time.
4. Teaching—How can teachers share their ideas, their activities and observe each other to disseminate the artistry and effectiveness of each teacher beyond his/her own classroom? What inservice or resources can be made available so the teacher can systemat- ically learn, and incorporate in daily teaching, those basic princi- ples related to human learning which promote accomplishment of any academic, affective or psychomotor objective? So much is now known in the science of instruction that a teacher no longer need hope for independent learners. That outcome can predictably be achieved.

The dividends from such an investment of teacher time and energy? *Self-propelling lifelong learners and a teacher with a real sense of profes- sional contribution and accomplishment.*

For additional information:

Boight, Ralph Claud. *Invitation to Learning:* The Learning Center Handbook. Washington, D. C.: Acropolis Books, Ltd.

Lloyd, Dorothy M. *70 Activities for Classroom Learning Centers.* Dans- ville, N. Y. 14337. The Instructor Publications, Inc.

Platts, Mary E., and Sister Rose Marguerite. *SPICE, suggested activities to motivate the teaching of the language arts in the elementary schools*. Stevensville, Michigan: Educational Service, Inc., P.O. Box 219.

Rapport, Virginia and Parker, Mary. *Learning Center: Children on Their Own*. Washington, D. C.: Association for Childhood Education, 3615 Wisconsin Avenue, N. W.

Zacarias. *Fun and Games with Mathematics, Primary Book I*. Los Gatos, California: Contemporary Ideas, P.O. Box 1703.

Zacarias. *More Fun and Games, Primary Book II*. Los Gatos, California: Contemporary Ideas, P.O. Box 1703.

GIVING EFFECTIVE DIRECTIONS

MEETING PLAN

Long Range Objectives
Teachers will demonstrate proficiency in giving directions so they are easily and accurately followed by students.

Students will demonstrate attending behavior (looking and listening carefully) when directions are given and be accountable for accurate performance.

Staff Meeting Objectives
Teachers will discuss factors that promote successful direction giving and practice giving and analyzing directions for rainy day games and indoor activities.

Teachers will develop a file of games and activities with well designed directions.

Teachers will apply their knowledge about giving successful directions to all directions given to students.

Preparation for Staff Meeting
Teachers should have the opportunity to read "The Science of the Art of giving Directions" on page 97. If this is not possible, the principal or a designated staff member should present the content of that section at the beginning of the staff meeting. Each step should be listed on the chalkboard as meaning is developed and examples are given.

The principal or specified members of the staff should be prepared to present examples of written and oral directions for group analysis.

Staff Discussion
Excellent practice in sharpening directions occurs as staff members analyze the strengths and ambiguities in each set of directions given as an example by the group leader.

Examples:

1. "Read the directions on the board and follow them. I'll see who is able to do it."

   Get your paper ready—
   First and last name—top line on left
   Date—top line on right
   Number each line below your name from 1–10

2. "Get anything you need, sharpen your pencils and start to work." (When there is only one pencil sharpener, few sources of materials and misunderstanding of what is to be done, a stampede is generated.)

It is important to note that there is a great deal to be learned from analyzing directions that are deliberately made confusing in order to pinpoint the reasons those directions were unsuccessful and how they can be corrected. It also is laugh provoking and therapeutic to give a poor set of directions "on purpose."

After the elements of successful directions are identified and examples given, someone should have prepared in advance, an example of directions for a rainy day game so those directions can be given to see if the members of the staff can follow them correctly.

Here is a Sample Indoor Game, "Find the Missing Object."

The leader selects some small object (earring, block, eraser, etc.,) and places it in the room where it is not easily seen, but can be located without moving any other object (tucked by a book, close to the eraser in the chalk tray, by the leg of a chair). All students walk around the room searching with their eyes. When a student locates the object, he pretends to look in two additional places so as not to signal the correct location to others and then he sits down. Each student continues to search until he locates the object.

This is a high interest, "moving about" game that gives students a stretch but maintains quiet and order.

Directions to Students

"Let's see what good detectives you are. I have placed an object like this (show similar earring, block, eraser, etc.,) in this room where you can see it without touching or moving anything."

"Your job is to walk around with your hands in back of you until you locate the object with your eyes. Then look at two more places so

94

no one knows where you found it and then go to your seat.

"Suppose I had placed it here," (leader places the similar object). "Watch how I will look for it," (leader demonstrates moving about with hands clasped in back until (s)he sees it). "Now that I have found it, what must I do?" (This will emphasize looking in two more places before sitting down, the most difficult part of the directions.)

The leader will need to determine if it is necessary to have a student also model the behavior, including looking at two more places.

"All right, let's see if you can find the object I really hid, and remember what to do after you locate it."

It will give the participants in the staff meeting a stretch and develop interest if they actually play the game.

Other staff members should be encouraged to share some of their most successful rainy day games and give the directions as a model of the elements of successful direction giving that have been discussed.

Follow-up

Following the staff meeting, the principal and staff should monitor their own direction giving as well as be on the alert for opportunities (assemblies, cafeteria and other school procedures, etc.,) to design good directions and monitor the success of the students following directions.

To develop a repertoire of rainy day games and activities, each staff member might prepare a set of directions for one activity or game. These can be "taught" to the total staff at a subsequent meeting to show concrete evidence of the quality of the directions as the staff members successfully engage in the activity. If mistakes and misunderstandings occur, directions need to be revised. Staff members also can suggest ways to make the activity more difficult for mature learners or easier for less advanced students. The game of Twenty Questions is one of many examples that can be adapted to any level.

When directions are refined so they are easily followed, the games or activities with directions can be duplicated for each staff member so precious meeting time is spent on professional discussion and decisions rather than note taking, and each teacher will have a file of rainy day games.

Principal's Responsibility

The principal in routine classroom visits should notice teachers' direction giving and reinforce successful application of the content of the staff meeting as well as assist the teacher when help is needed. Teachers should be encouraged to learn from each other by being relieved for an occasional 15–20 minutes to visit other classrooms as well as to discuss and share with each other their successful and unsuccessful direction giving.

The principal should also model direction giving in his directions to staff, students, bulletins, parent communications. Excellence and clarity will result from a deliberate effort to improve directions.

Dividends

The professional growth of the total staff in giving directions will be amazing. "The kids listen better" will be the inevitable comment. "The staff gives better directions" will be the reality.

THE SCIENCE OF THE ART OF GIVING DIRECTIONS

"They simply cannot follow directions," is to education what the common cold is to medicine. Everyone is complaining about it. Every classroom has a problem with it. It's seldom fatal, but in terms of time, energy, and productivity, the resulting loss is astronomical.

Science has not yet solved the problem of the common cold. Application of what science has discovered about how to give directions, *however,* will go a long way towards curing that classroom malady.

As we study the etiology of students' *not* following directions, we find there are three common causes:

1. *The student does not intend to follow directions.* The direction, "Go directly to your play area," which is followed by the student detouring to enjoy a water fight in the lavatory is an example of a student choosing not to follow directions which clearly (s)he understands and could follow if (s)he wished.

2. *The student is incapable of following the direction.* "Don't be nervous when you stand up to speak," is a typical example. (When was the last time someone told you not to worry and *you* stopped?) Not so obvious, but equally illustrative are the directions and school assignments given to students who have not yet learned the necessary skills. No matter how hard they try, they cannot follow such directions.

3. *The directions themselves, or the method of giving directions, has built-in power to confuse or make unclear.* An income tax form is an example which is only too familiar. Unfortunately, because direction giving is an only recently articulated skill, countless directions which generate predictable confusion are given daily.

Of the three reasons for failure to follow directions, lack of necessary skills and confusing directions indicate a change must be made by the teacher so (s)he applies what is now known about human learning to the achievement at successful directions. While reason number one clearly involves a change in attitude of the learner so (s)he intends to follow the directions, this too can usually be accomplished with the application of the principles of motivation on page 31.

The writer recognizes the fact that there are many times when the teacher need not give directions; the learner should be directing his own behavior. At other times, it is essential to give directions that will facilitate learning, as well as to teach the skill of "following directions" which will be needed throughout the student's life. "When all else fails, follow the directions," is an admonition that often is appropriate.

So the teacher will develop skills in direction giving, this chapter will focus primarily on reason three, the "built-in" success or failure power of the directions themselves and the way they are given. The teacher, however, must always consider the questions: (1) Is the student really trying to follow the directions: and (2) Is (s)he able to follow them if (s)he tries?

Directions involve two basic steps:

1. Planning—thinking through the directions in advance to determine:
   a. How many different things must the student remember to do?
   b. Which of these has (s)he done before and which are new?
   c. Can (s)he do the new things if (s)he tries?
   d. How many directions must be given at one time?
   e. When is the best time to give these directions?
   f. What is the best sequence for several directions that must be given at the same time?
   g. Should the directions be written or verbal?
   h. Will special help be necessary for certain students?

Out of these considerations an operational plan evolves.

2. Giving directions (to an individual or a group):
   a. Getting attention.
   b. Giving the directions in a way that reflects conscious planning.
   c. Checking understanding.
   d. Modeling.
   e. Translating into student action.
   f. Redirecting if necessary.

Successful direction-giving becomes an automatic synthesis of all these elements, but a success-oriented approach involves considering each separately to determine how best to accomplish that element. Such professional analysis makes it possible to pinpoint an error and remediate that part in order to promote success. In short, an analytic approach enables teachers to systematically learn at a conscious level (not blind imitation) how to give directions. If directions are not followed, it is possible to identify what went wrong and adjust that part rather than practice random trial and error tinkering.

I. Planning

It is essential that we break complex behavior into parts. Getting ready for recess involves the possibility of disposition of finished and/or unfinished work, clearing desks and tables, putting away supplies, being at the appropriate place to be excused, putting on wraps, and knowing where to go when excused.

Eventually the direction, "Get ready for recess," should trigger all these behaviors, but only if each element has previously been learned, which means it *must have been taught.*

In the same way, "Go to the library," "Read the chapter and answer the questions," "Pass in your papers," "Come to the discussion circle," represent composites of simpler directions, each one of which must be learned.

How Many Directions?

A simple rule of thumb is that probably not more than three directions should be given at the same time. If the behavior required by any one direction is new or not well learned, that direction should be given alone or paired with a well-learned behavior. Seldom (if ever!) should directions for two new behaviors be given at the same time. Often complex behaviors can be broken into several sets of directions with one set being accomplished before the next is given. If more than three directions must be given, these can be written or in a picture graph for easy reference by the student.

Timing and Sequence

A decision made in advance of *when* directions should be given can contribute immeasurably to success. Delaying directions for an activity until just before that activity is to be performed eliminates a great deal of forgetting and confusion. The time to give directions for what to do when you come into the room tomorrow morning is not when you come into the room *this* morning. Those directions for tomorrow should be given just before dismissal today or, possibly, tomorrow morning so they can be followed immediately. This is assuming, of course, that following directions is the major objective, rather than the objective of assuming the responsibility for remembering over a period of time. The latter also is an important objective, but the teaching strategy to achieve *remembering* would be different.

An example of ending a sequence of directions with the direction to be followed immediately is, "After recess today we will go to the auditorium instead of coming back to our room; now check your papers to see if you wish to turn them in or keep them; and excuse yourself for recess as soon as you're ready." Such a set of directions implies the learners have had the experience of going directly to the auditorium and know what to do when they get there, they know the criteria that determine whether or not papers are finished, and they have had experience excusing themselves. If any one of these is a new behavior, beware—for catastrophe is imminent!

Individualizing

Even in direction-giving, individualization of instruction is essential for there will always be those for whom the direction may be too difficult to be accomplished independently. Anticipating these situations in advance makes it possible for a teacher to give help yet maintain the dignity of such students. "Let's see, Bill, how many have you finished? Do you have more to do? Then where will you put your paper?" enables a student who could not function independently to follow directions successfully.

It is interesting to note that we are well aware that some students will need extra assistance in reading, writing, and math, but we do not offer them that same support in following directions, no matter how vividly they indicate their need. "If they would only LISTEN!" is our panacea.

Written or Oral?

Whether directions should be written or oral is determined by the students' need to "read and do" or "listen and do." Both skills are important, but a well-planned set of written directions often provides needed practice for the student because (s)he must read, comprehend, and transform his understanding into performance. Also, it avoids the necessity for repetition and questions because (s)he has something to refer to. Even young children can follow picture directions of (1) a lunch box or sack, (2) a door, (3) lips closed, which signify get your lunch and wait quietly at the door. The vividness of such directions often is more effective than an adult's voice which many have learned to ignore.

Thinking through directions in advance will enable a teacher to determine how many should be given at one time, those directions which may be difficult or impossible for some students, the order in which to give those directions, and whether they should be written or oral.

Automating

At this point the reader may exclaim, "With all the directions I have to give every day, who has time for all this thinking through?" The answer is "Nobody," but practicing thinking through some directions provides training in direction-giving so it becomes an automatic skill in the same way that practicing certain skills in driving soon makes them automatic. Successful achievement of your purpose is the result of both kinds of practice.

II. Giving the Directions

The first requisite for following directions is to understand them which requires conscious effort and attention to the source of the directions. Consequently, the first step of direction-giving is to gain the attention of those who must receive the message. Teachers need to deliberately and systematically develop some method whereby *all* the learners for whom the directions are intended are focused on the source of information. One of the most common causes of failure is that the teacher gives directions when not all of the group is listening or looking. Teaching students to stop work and look up at an agreed upon signal is a sine qua non of a successful classroom.

Giving Directions as Planned

When the teacher gives planned directions (s)he will reap the reward of professional effort. Children will put their lunches away and *then* hang up their wraps, rather than wrestling with jackets, trying to hang on to lunches or having them trampled by other children in the same fix. Students will have heard or be able to read what to do when they come into the room rather than losing precious time in confusion. An unexpected change in plans or schedule can be dealt with in an orderly and productive way rather than the change destroying classroom equilibrium.

Checking Understanding

Unfortunately, giving directions well does not *guarantee* they have been understood. To ensure that directions will be followed, the teacher must check understanding. "Think of what you will do first. If you know, raise your hand." Then the teacher must WAIT, nudging with his/her eyes those students who have no intention of "putting their minds in gear." Such teaching makes clear to students that they are

101

accountable for listening and identifies for the teacher those who don't know what to do. If only a few hands go up, the teacher has evidence that directions are not understood and they must be regiven either by children or teacher. If most hands are up, the teacher will decide whether those who don't know can be told by other children or need teacher remedial attention. The entire set of directions must be checked. If this takes too much time it will alert the teacher to the fact that there may have been too many directions.

Modeling the Behavior

Recent brain research has corroborated classroom experience that indicates some students learn easier by hearing, some by reading, and some by seeing. Whenever possible, we must provide for the latter group by having a student model the behavior. This also provides correction for possible misunderstanding. "John, show us what you will do first." "Mary, pretend you have finished; show us where you will put your paper." "Tom, show us where you will get your materials." "Jane, should you need help, show us what you will do."

This modeling is effective for others only if it has their conscious attention. "Let's watch John and decide if he is following the new directions. Thumbs up if you think he is." Insist that each student make a judgment. Above all, avoid the error of "Sally, did John follow directions?" The minute you say "Sally" before you ask the question, it signals the group that no one else will have to think.

Translating Into Action

When directions have been given, comprehension checked, and behavior modeled, the teacher must decide if all children, or a few at a time will proceed. "If you know what to do you may start; if you're not sure, stay with me (or raise your hand) and I will help you," is a strategy that will not delay those who are ready but will provide assistance for those who need it.

The teacher needs also to consider whether the total class can get their books, wraps, lunches, or get started on the assignment at the same time. Usually the "pile ups" that occur can be avoided by releasing a few children while the rest are doing something appropriate (*not* just sitting and waiting). "Be deciding on what you are going to write about (or color or choose) and I'll ask you to tell me as I excuse you," will start students towards purposeful thinking while they are waiting.

These precious minutes of waiting time also can be sopped up by the Sponge activities described on page 76.

Remediating

With the best of directions, occasionally there remains the child who doesn't follow them. If there are many such children, either the directions have been inappropriate or poorly given or the motivation variables listed on page 31 should have been incorporated. After releasing children to follow directions, the teacher must take a few minutes to check who is following them and who isn't. We check arithmetic papers to see who can do the problems and who can't, don't we? Otherwise, how would we know who needs help? In the same way we find out who needs help with the directions and why. "Bill, what do you need to do first? Where would you go to get it? Show me," helps the uncertain child to learn what to do. *Telling him again only repeats a teaching action that we have evidence did not work.*

The Science of Giving Directions

Let's review what is needed for a good set of directions.

Planning: Think through the directions. Decide how many are needed at one time. Determine the order and whether they will be written or oral. Anticipate which students will need help.

Implementation: Get the attention of the students, give the directions, check comprehension, and model the behavior. Release students so it is possible for them to efficiently perform. Check to see who needs help and give it in a way that enables that student to learn.

The Art of Giving Directions

Once a teacher knows the science of giving directions, that knowledge becomes the launching pad for artistry in teaching. The vividness and interesting quality of directions, professional decisions about which child needs the experience or status of modeling for the class, decisions about how soon students can become their own direction-givers, the quality and value of the learning task for which directions are given—these are the hallmarks of the artist in teaching. The science of direction-giving we can put on paper. The artistry must be your own.

USING AIDES/VOLUNTEERS
IN THE CLASSROOM

MEETING PLAN

Long Range Objective

Teachers, aides/volunteers will become a productive classroom team using vocabulary, concepts and strategies which will increase students' learning and which are understood by all team members.

Staff Meeting Objectives

Teachers will identify categories of tasks which are appropriate for aides/volunteers.

Teachers will plan inservice activities that enable aides/volunteers to become skilled in each of those tasks.

Teachers will plan inservice activities that enable teachers to delegate appropriate classroom responsibilities and increase the performance skill of aides/volunteers.

Preparation for Staff Meeting

Throughout the country, parents and other adults are becoming involved in aide/volunteer service in the classroom. These people constitute a powerful, previously untapped resource which promises relief to an over-taxed and understaffed educational program.

There is, however, a danger inherent in this assistance, for a myth exists that any extra body is of use in the classroom. Findings to date indicate this is not so. If an aide/volunteer has *learned* to work productively with children and a teacher has *learned* to use an aide/volunteer as an adjunct to an educational program, a productive relationship emerges. If, however, inappropriate responsibilities are given to the aide/volunteer, or if teacher and aide/volunteer work in competition rather than cooperation, educational disaster is likely. To avert this unhappy outcome, decisions about activities and responsibilities must be made in advance and inservice for both aides/volunteers and teachers must be provided. Indentification of appropriate and satisfying responsibilities, and planning an inservice program to enable all parties to fulfill these responsibilities should be the outcome of this staff meeting. Subsequent teacher interaction with aides/volunteers should result in harmonious teamwork, where both teachers and aides/volunteers will have realistic expectations for themselves and for each other.

Prior to the staff meeting, teachers should receive the following questions so they can be thinking about and generating answers:

1. What tasks, not involving children, could an aide/volunteer perform in your classroom?
2. What tasks involving children, could an aide/volunteer perform in your classroom?
3. What knowledge and skills must an aide/volunteer have in order to perform each of those tasks competently?
4. How can the teacher and aide/volunteer systematically and effectively communicate?

To initiate thinking, the following outline may be helpful:

1. Tasks not involving work with children:
   a. Preparation and housekeeping in the classroom (securing materials, reorganizing cupboards).
   b. Clerical (typing, dittoing).
   c. Record keeping for the teacher (correcting and/or recording children's work).
2. Tasks involving work with children:
   a. Reading or telling stories.
   b. Assisting children to practice reading, writing, math, etc.
   c. Yard and lunch assistance.
   d. Supervision in the classroom.
   e. Utilization of special skills of aide/volunteer—art projects, music, drama, sports.

If teachers on the staff have learned the skills to do so, the knowledge and skills needed by an aide/volunteer should be stated in behavioral terms rather than as a general trait. "Patience" is better described as "working without any sign of irritation or hurry when a student is confused or needs to go over something again." "Help in reading" means a cluster of skills. Each needs to be made explicit. For example: "The aide/volunteer can identify under what conditions (s)he would a) tell the student the unknown word, b) have him seek context clues, c) use phonics, or d) give him other kinds of assistance," specifies one skill needed by the aide/volunteer if (s)he is to work with a student.

Staff Discussion

At the staff meeting, the teachers should begin by listing on a chalkboard those tasks not involving children, because this is the easiest of the four questions to answer. Whoever chairs the meeting will need to keep the teachers focused on the listing of those tasks, for everyone will want to discuss the other questions at the same time and the result will be the typical "meeting muddle."

Next the group should list tasks involving children. There will be problems for the group will want to debate each issue. The leader must insist on merely listing possibilities. Whether or not a task is appropriate depends on the aide/volunteer's possession of skills necessary to its performance and the identification of that knowledge and those skills is the answer to the third question.

To answer the third question, the staff should divide into small groups where debate is possible. (It's a waste of time with the total staff.) Some teachers may choose the easier task of identification of skills needed for responsibilities not involving students, other staff members will tackle the difficult identification of skills necessary to supervise lunch benches, assist in practice of reading or number combinations, read a story to the entire class, give words needed in creative writing, etc. The other staff meetings in this book will provide additional background for the analysis of skills needed.

Each small group should list its conclusions in writing. This not only tightens thinking and discussion, but the formation can be duplicated for consideration and refinement by the entire staff.

If there is time at this meeting, suggestions should be elicited for systematic, effective and satisfying communication between teacher and aide/volunteer. Too often, this is left to chance with haphazard, unsatisfying results. Notebooks, places on the bulletin board, once a week conferences, can go far toward the alleviation of this potential problem.

If there is not enough time to discuss techniques for satisfying communication, this problem should be the focus of a subsequent meeting.

Follow-up

It is highly unlikely that small groups will finish at the initial meeting. This is as it should be, for a week of consideration and informal discussion will result in responses of higher quality. Also, as skills are identified, plans need to be made for inservice, and persons need to be identified who will take on the important task of training the aides/

volunteers usually for several sessions.° To have each teacher do all the training of his/her own aide/volunteer is wasteful of time and energy. Scheduling an inservice group for all aides/volunteers will result in their learning from each other as well as from the group leader. The teacher to whom the aide/volunteer is then assigned can expect to receive a teammate who is equipped with basic skills and who needs help only in extending, refining, and adapting those skills to the routines of a particular classroom.

An essential beginning of any program for aides/volunteers is observation in many classrooms in the school, not just the one where an individual will be working, so this overview should be built into the training program. It is essential that aides/volunteers observe as a group accompanied by the principal or a staff member who can interpret what is seen. Observation without interpretation as to why a teacher is dong what (s)he is doing is not only useless, it actually can be detrimental, as erroneous assumptions are made or successful teacher actions are imitated by the aide/volunteer in situations where those actions are not appropriate.

Principal's Responsibility

The principal has the responsibility for monitoring the training program for aides/volunteers and it is desirable that (s)he conduct some of the inservice sessions. (S)he should design one session which spells out the role and responsibility (legal and educational) of a paraprofessional in that school. Also, aides/volunteers need to understand the functions of office staff, nurse, guidance workers, etc.

The principal has the subsequent responsibility, unless (s)he delegates it to an aide/volunteer chairperson, to monitor the "fit" of teacher to aide/volunteer, making sure that responsibilities are appropriate and fulfilled. At times, (s)he may need to become an arbitrator or make a change in assignment to restore equilibrium.

Subsequent meetings with teachers and aides/volunteers will demonstrate the principal's interest in the program and identify any tension points so they can be resolved. Identification of successful teamwork between teacher-aide/volunteer, can also serve as a model for future inservice. The principal's interest in and reindorcement of productive

---

°A packaged inservice program, "Aide-ing in Education" with discussion guides, films and written materials is listed at the end of this section.

programs and relationships will go far toward assuring the success of the entire program.

Dividends

Teaching is a highly complex profession and knowledge is rapidly accumulating which makes students' successful learning more predictable. As teachers transmit some of their skills to an aide/volunteer, those skills, once articulated and examined, become increasingly refined and result in increased professional competence of all adults throughout the school.

Having competent aides/volunteers in the classroom will free the teacher for more highly professional and creative activities which will enhance the entire educational program.

For additional information:

Books:

Hunter, Madeline. *Aide-ing in Education.* A series of ten one hour inservice meetings with a book of meeting plans, reading material plus accompanying inservice films. TIP Publications, P.O. Box 514, El Segundo, California 90245.

Films:

"Welcome Back to School." color. 30 minutes.

"Increasing Students' Motivation to Learn." color. 30 minutes.

"Increasing Productive Behavior." color. 30 minutes.

"Motivation and Reinforcement in the Classroom." color. 30 minutes.

"Extending Students' Thinking." color. 30 minutes.

"Reading a Story to Extend Thinking." color. 30 minutes.

"Improving Practice." color. 30 minutes.

"Helping in Reading." color. 30 minutes.

"Helping in Math." color. 30 minutes.

"The Aide in the Classroom." color. 30 minutes.

SPECIAL PURPOSE FILMS
26740 Latigo Shore Drive
Malibu, California 90265

SUGGESTED AIDE/VOLUNTEER
RESPONSIBILITIES *

How teachers can best use aide/volunteers is determined by the competency of the aide/volunteer, the needs of the students and by the creativity of the teacher. To determine responsibilities appropriate for a particular situation, it may be helpful to look at four categories of possible teacher assistance.

1. Preparation and Housekeeping

2. Clerical Work

3. Record Keeping

4. Working wth Children

Some responsibility for assisting in each of these categories makes a more interesting assignment. To enrich and extend the learning in a classroom, opportunities should be planned where the aide/volunteer can share his/her unique skills and talents: musical, culinary, artistic, scientific, needlework and even collections from butons to stamps. Creativity and sensitivity to the needs of aides/volunteers, students and teachers will produce a rich program.

The following is a check list of possible responsibilities for aides/ volunteers, to which should be added the particular assignments needed in each classroom:

Preparation and Housekeeping
- — Make teaching aids, such as games, flashcards.
- — Set up for learning activities and centers.
- — Prepare materials, such as cutting paper, sharpening pencils.
- — Replenish supplies that are low.
- — Maintain art supplies by washing paint brushes, filling water containers, (mixing paints, clay, etc.).
- — Prepare milk or snack.
- — Help to care for plants, animals.
- — See that cupboards, table tops, storage spaces, counters, etc. are neat and ready for use.

Clerical
- — Prepare dittos and stencils.
- — Run duplicating machines.

*Developed in collaboration with Sally Breit, Supervisor, University Elementary School.

— Operate audio/visual equipment.
— Type as needed.
— Make phone calls as needed.
— Secure films and books from storage.
— File materials.
— Put names of students on roll, lists, materials.
— Correct Students' Work.

Record Keeping
— Record attendance.
— Record behavior of children.
— Record students' work.
— Maintain records of milk money, lunch money, etc.
— Inventory and reorder as needed.

Work with Children
In small groups and/or one to one:
— Practice in math, reading spelling, writing.
— Write and/or type dictated stories.
— Talk with children for their language practice, including bilingual children.
— Read Stories.
— Supervise a listening or learning center.
— Sing with children.
— Play an instrument.
— Assist with an art experience.
— Assist with a cooking or other hobby experience.
— Help a group move from one place to another, such as classroom to lunchroom, library, auditorium.
— Play/teach games in classroom and on play yard.
— Share hobbies, interests and collections.
— Accompany group on field trips.
In larger groups:
— Read a story.
— Monitor children working on assignments.
— Assist class in library.
— Supervise lunchroom.
— Supervise play yard.
— Assist at dismissal, with crossing guard, etc.

IMPROVING PARENT CONFERENCES

MEETING PLAN

Long Range Objective

Responses from parents and teachers will indicate increased skill with, and satisfaction from parent conferences as the objectives of information getting, information giving and problem solving are more successfully achieved.

Meeting Objectives

These objectives will require more than one session.
The staff will:

1. Identify the three purposes of parent conferences and list one student in their classrooms for which each type of conference would be indicated.
2. Discuss the components of (a) preparing for the conference, (b) holding the conference and (c) evaluating the conference.
3. Role play each of the three kinds of conferences and discuss the enabling as well as the interfering factors that emerge.
4. Develop a procedure so, prior to attending the conference, parents can identify their primary concerns or priorities for information desired.

Preparation for Staff Meeting

Before the staff meeting, teachers should have the opportunity to think through and discuss informally the answers to the following questions:

1. Why have a parent conference? What can be accomplished there that cannot be communicated by a report card?
2. What are diferent purposes for holding a parent conference?
3. What perceivable evidence would a teacher use to determine if a parent conference had been successful?
4. What can the teacher do if there is lack of communication?

5. What responsibilities should the student have for preparation, participation and evaluation of the conference about him/her?

Prior to the meeting, teachers should have the opportunity to read the section on "Improving Parent Conferencing" in this book. If that is not possible, at the beginning of the meeting the principal or a staff member should present to the group the information contained in the section. Outlining of main points on a chalkboard or distributing a short (1–2 page) summary of the content to be used as a reference during the meeting is helpful.

Staff Discussion

The discussion should include:
1. Parent conferences and report cards in terms of their ability to communicate accurately.
2. The three purposes for holding a conference.
3. Preparation for a successful conference.
4. Students' responsibilities in parent conferencing.
5. Factors that promote successful communication.
6. Evidence of success, or lack of it, of the conference.

Because parent conferences can be an emotion laden subject, it will be difficult for the chairperson to keep the group focused on one area at a time as each staff member will want to contribute in the area of his greatest concern. It will help if the topics are listed on a chalkboard and group members' responses are labeled as to the category in which they belong. It may be necessary to jot down comments and questions and delay discussion of them until that category is reached.

At the end of the meeting each teacher should list the three purposes of parent conferences and one student or situation for which each purpose is appropriate. These will become the practice areas for implementation of the knowledge and techniques discussed in the meeting.

Suggested procedures should be developed whereby the parent, prior to the conference, can express concerns or priorities for information desired. Teachers should be encouraged to try these procedures and report back on their effectiveness and suggestions for improving them.

Follow-up

At a subsequent meeting, volunteer staff members can role play conferences of their three examples. The group will then identify enabling and interfering factors that occurred and suggest alternative strategies.

Staff members will realize greater ease and insight as they assume both teacher's and parent's role in a simulated conference. Deliberately

112

doing some "wrong things" highlights common problems and eliminates the strain of role playing a "perfect conference." There's a lot of fun, "therapy" and learning when a teacher assumes the role of a difficult parent. Teachers also can develop facility with enabling phrases such as "I am puzzled," "help me to understand," "let me see if I understand" and sensitivity to phrases that need to be avoided such as "we think you should," "your child has a problem," "you can't hold us responsible."

It is an excellent morale boosting experience and provides rich learning dividends if the principal, or a staff member other than the student's teacher prepares to hold a conference on a particular student. If that student's real teacher then plays the role of the parent (which often can be done with authenticity), it enables the teacher to "taste" the experience of both parties at the conference. Real empathy and understanding can be generated by this technique.

Informal reporting back to the staff and/or principal of parent conference experiences will deepen perception and develop evaluative insight. The principal may wish to request from each teacher a list of the five most successful conferences, as evaluated by the teacher and two conferences with which the teacher was not well satisfied.

The Principal's Responsibilities

The principal is a powerful model for his teachers so (s)he should demonstrate these same conferencing techniques in principal-teacher conferences. Determining whether the primary purpose of the principal-teacher conference is to give information, get information or solve a problem, and letting the teacher know that purpose at the beginning of the conference will result in a great deal of observational learning by the teacher. The principal should examine the degree to which it is reasonable that the purpose can be achieved in one conference and anticipate the need for data and follow-up in the same way (s)he expects teachers to utilize those skills in parent conferencing.

It also is the responsibility of the principal to see that parents have an opportunity to learn how to participate with increased skill and satisfaction in a parent-teacher conference. A workshop for a pilot group of volunteer parents can be conducted by school staff using much the same format as that used in the staff meeting. After the pilot workshop, the leaders can conduct workshops at PTA meetings, grade level meetings, etc.

It is helpful if the principal occasionally "sits in" on parent conferences to experience the general climate of parent conferencing in the school. (S)he also should join the teacher as a "conference team member" in difficult conferences or when apprehension or dissatisfaction has been expressed by either party.

Dividends

The dividends from improved home-school communication cannot be over estimated. Children who are productively learning with the support of both teachers and parents, and parents who are fully informed partners in the educational enterprise constitute the most desirable end product of education. There is no better public relations program to ensure productive and enthusiastic public support of education.

DEVELOPING PROFICIENCY IN
PARENT CONFERENCES *

Giving parents more *meaningful* information about how their child is doing in school has resulted in a significant increase in parent conferences. Sensitivity to the need for getting helpful information *from* parents and co-operatively making decisions and working out educational solutions to students' problems has also contributed to this increase.

Parent-teacher conferences have always been held. In the past, however, those that did not deal with a problem ("I'm going to have to see your parents"), often were informal or happenstance at PTA meetings, in the hall or in grocery stores. Now, more and more school districts are designating the parent conference as an official report of student progress.

Efforts to achieve more meaningful communication with parents evolved because the formal procedure of a report card or check list could do little more than label categories in which a student fell ("doing well" "needs to improve") or convey a terse message by a phrase or comment. This no longer is satisfying to either teacher or parent, both are seeking ways to increase home-school communication.

In their preservice training, many teachers have had little or no preparation for the sensitive task of conducting a productive conference. Consequently, success or lack of it often is dependent on intuitive abilities rather than the systematic acquisition of conferencing skills which are sharpened by guided practice.

Some parent-teacher conferences are relatively simple to conduct (after all, we do have successful students, marvelous parents and superb teachers). Some conferences, however, take place under emotionally stressful conditions and can have far reaching consequences in terms of students' success in school, parents' feelings about school, public support of education, and teachers' professional satisfaction.

Fortunately, a conference is similar to teaching in that (1) it requires planning, (2) it has an identified purpose, (3) facts and ideas need to be validly communicated, (4) principles affecting human learning operate in the interaction between teacher and parent, and (5) there is an outcome which can be evaluated in terms of the behavior of

*This article was prepared in collaboration with Gerda Lawrence, MSW who brings interviewing theory to the field of Education. Mrs. Lawrence is the clinical social worker at the University Elementary School, University of California, Los Angeles.

the participants. These similarities enable teachers to transfer a great deal of their teaching knowledge into conferencing skills.

Planning for the Conference
Every conference requires the following planning:

1. Identification of, and agreement between parent and teacher as to the main purpose of the conference. Everything cannot be achieved in one conference. Most of the conference time should be devoted to one primary purpose. Urgency of concern of either the teacher or parent determines priorities in use of conference time.
2. Estimation of the degree to which it is reasonable that this purpose be achieved in one conference. (Parents, like students, don't learn everything at once.)
3. Identification of the information and materials which should be available at the conference (anecdotal records, student's work, observations of the particular student's attitudes and behaviors by the teacher or by children and other staff members).
4. Determination of the student's role and responsibility in preparation, participation and evaluation of the conference.
5. Anticipation of parent response which could indicate whether successful or unsuccessful communication has occurred.
6. Anticipation of necessary follow-up to conference (phone calls, notes or written reports, time of next conference, etc.).

Purpose of the Conference
A conference will have one of the following as a basic purpose:

  I. Information giving
 II. Information getting
III. Problem solving

While activities in all three categories may occur in a single conference, one major purpose must be the priority if success and satisfaction are to result from a single meeting.

I. Information Giving Conferences
If the primary purpose of the conference is to give information, the teacher must determine the information most pertinent to the parent's question, "How is my child doing?" "Doing" can mean different things

116

to parent and teacher; that is why it is so important that a parent indicate areas of primary concern before the conference. Everything about the child cannot be included, nor should it be, for the items of real importance to parent and teacher must be highlighted, not lost in information of less importance. If the information is positive, most parents will receive it warmly. If some of the information is negative or emotion laden, the teacher must consider how the parent may best be able to "hear" the message and what is to be done if, at this time, the parent is unable to "receive" the negative information.

Questions the teacher must consider before conducting the information giving conference:

1. *What do I need to communicate and what do the parents want to know? What is of real importance or concern to them?* Often the latter can be ascertained before the conference by sending home a note or form asking, "What information do you want to make sure is included in your conference?" "What special questions do you have about your child?" When a possibly unwelcome message needs to be delivered, the teacher has the additional responsibility for sensitively selecting the words and phrases that best communicate it.

Examples of unwelcome messages are:

"Your child has a hard time controlling his behavior."

"Your child seems to find academic learning very difficult."

"Your child may not be interested in going to college."

"Your child finds it hard to finish a task."

"Your child has a difficult time with his classmates."

It is important to note that no one of us ever is omniscient enough to deliver the message, "Your child can't _____" (implying that he never will be able to). Neither teacher nor parent can validly make such an unqualified statement. It is better to deliver such a message by phrasing it so that it states objective observations while indicating that changes can occur ("At this time your child is not. . . ." or "Your child has not yet learned to. . . .")

Some parents are aware of the situation and will be relieved by the honesty of the teacher. At other times it may be necessary to spend time to enable the parents, by means of objective data (anecdotal records, child's work), to see the problem for themselves.

2. *How will the teacher know if the parent has "heard" the message or received the information?* Usually, a "playback" by the parent

117

at the end of the conference will reveal understanding or mis-understanding. Questions such as, "Would you briefly summarize what you heard me say so I know I have said it clearly?" or "What parts of your child's progress are most satisfying and on what parts should we both work?" can generate the needed evidence.

3. *What is the student's role and responsibility in preparing, conducting and evaluating the conference with his parents?* Will the student and/or you determine his/her role? Increasingly, it is seen as appropriate that students have some control of and responsibility for communication of information which concerns them. Students should assist in the data gathering which is a preparation for the conference. Their perceptions of how they are doing, their strengths and accomplishments, as well as their needs to improve, constitute information which students should be aware of, articulate, and directly confront. Whether or not they assume responsibility for the presentation of this information to their parents is a question which they and their teachers jointly answer. It can be a growth experience for a student to present to a "significant other" his/her preceptions of his/her assets and liabilities, successes and plans for future accomplishments. It can also be a tension producing experience requiring maturity and objectivity which could be beyond the present capacities of some learners (and possibly some parents!).

4. *What follow-up is needed after the conference?* If some desired information is not available, how, when and by whom will it be ascertained and delivered? What will determine when the next conference is scheduled who will assume the responsibility for initiating it and what follow-up information will be included? What is the student's responsibility for delivering information between home and school before the next conference? If recommendations are made, how will they be recorded and who will have the responsibility for carrying them out?

II. Information Getting Conferences

At the first of the year, or in a puzzling situation, the primary purpose of a parent conference may be to secure information.

Questions the teacher must consider before an information getting conference:

1. *What information is needed?* The teacher must anticipate which

categories of information might be helpful in planning for the student, such as his feelings about school, his relevant past experiences and present out of school experiences, etc. The teacher also must alert herself to avoid receiving irrelevant information which is time consuming and nonproductive. Examples of nonproductive information are gossip, blaming in-laws or previous school experiences, extraneous information which may be interesting but is not helpful and which could be used by the parent as a way of avoidance or defense against confronting the present problem or situation.

2. *How will the parent know, before the conference, the areas where information is being sought?* Giving advance notice of the purpose of the conference and the areas of concern that will be discussed enables a parent to think through, secure, and possibly organize relevant information before being asked to present it.

3. *What records of the conference are needed?* Determination must be made by the teacher of how important information and agreements for action will be recorded so they are not forgotten. Will taking notes during the conference compliment the parent with a feeling of the importance of what is being communicated or distress her by the permanence of what is said? Jotting down notes at the end of the conference is one way to insure that important information or promised actions are not forgotten or misunderstood. These notes can become important beginnings for future communication and they also insure that parent and teacher agree as to what has been said and planned. ("Let's summarize the important points we have covered.")

4. *What are the student's responsibilities for supplying initial information?* Is the parent to be the first source of the information sought or will the parent conference be a follow-up to a teacher-student conference where areas needing further information or action have already been identified? ("Bill, let's list the things that have happened that make it hard for you to _____.")

III. Problem Solving Conference

This conference can be originated by either parent or teacher to generate action which will diminish or solve an *identified* problem (not to discuss general undefined concerns or vague issues). The problem may be an academic one such as a program for remediation or accelera-

119

tion, or a non-academic problem such as inability to make friends, tardiness, or lack of enthusiasm for school.

Questions the teacher needs to consider before the conference:

1. *What positive actions can be taken by the school to help the situation?* In preparing for a problem solving conference, the teacher first must focus on what the school can do. *No matter how remiss the parent or debilitating is the out of school environment, the teacher must resist the temptation to assume the school can do nothing until the out of school situation is remedied.* With effort by the school, the probability of parent cooperation is increased. A well met educational challenge usually yields in-school strategies that can aid the situation. Here the principal or guidance person has the responsibility for becoming an ally or a consultant in the generation and execution of a productive plan. That plan *must* be put into operation before a parent conference so the resultant growth (or lack of growth) can be an important practical source of information for the development of additional plans.

2. *What positive actions can be taken by the family to help the situation?* Only *after* the school has accepted responsibility for some positive in-school action with documented consequences, can the parent be expected to assume a part of the shared responsibility. Both teacher and parent must make sure that plans of either school or home are realistic in terms of time, skills, and energy constraints. Often both parties get carried away by the temptation of "a new start" and set unrealistic expectations which are doomed to fizzle out. Realistic plans, while less ambitious, have a better chance of implementation, consistency and survival so those plans will yield more student gain in the long run. From knowledge of the home situation, a teacher often can anticipate the strengths in the parents that are available to assist in the solution of the problem. Teaching parents the skills necessary to effect desirable changes is also a productive possibility.

3. *What follow-up is necessary to make sure plans are put into effect and are producing desired results?* We cannot expect a parent will "learn" just by being told once how to do something differently even if this "something" is no more than rearranging her use of time so that the child is not tardy in the morning. "Time to learn, and practice that learning" applies to parents as well as to students.

Conducting the Conference

The same principles which affect learning in the classroom operate in the interaction between teacher and parent. Parents will be influenced by the six factors listed in the section on motivation on page 31. Parent's productive behavior will respond to the use of positive reinforcement discussed on page 11. Parents need opportunities for effective practice as described on page 58.

As with any teaching, many parent responses cannot be predicted in advance and the teacher must be able to "think on her seat" in the conference. Material that will help the teacher to develop additional professional skills in conducting parent conferences is available.

Judging the Success of the Conference

While standardized evaluation techniques for parent conferences have not, as yet, been developed, it is possible to use observable evidence to judge the success of communication and the outcomes of a parent conference.

Questions to consider are:

1. *Was the purpose of the conference achieved?*

   If the purpose was information giving, did the parent "playback" accurately the most important information that was given?

   If the purpose was information getting, did the teacher secure information that helped in understanding a puzzling situation?

   If the purpose was problem solving, did parent and teacher identify and list actions that each would take towards the solution of the problem?

2. *Was the feeling tone of the conference consonant with the purpose of the conference?*

   Did the parent verbally or nonverbally give evidence of satisfaction with the conference (though not necessarily with the information given or the situation related to the problem discussed)?

   If an unwelcome message was delivered, did the parent involve herself verbally or nonverbally in the discussion or was there an exaggerated reaction or repression of feelings and words?

   Was the teacher satisfied that the conference went reasonably well, or as well as could be expected under the circumstances? If, on reflection, additional thoughts occurred to her, did she follow-up with a phone call or note?

3. *Do the parents volunteer their feelings of satisfaction with or suggestions for improving conferences?*

Have parents attended workshops, provided by the school, on productive participation in conferences?

Does a parent survey, or a sampling of parent responses, indicate general support of and satisfaction with their conferences?

Do parents believe it worthwhile to release teachers during school time or to dismiss school early to facilitate the scheduling of conferences?

4. *Do the teachers feel they are growing in their professional skills of conferencing?*

The ability to communicate feelings, knowledge, plans, hopes and dreams is one of mankinds most distinguishing assets. The face to face communication possible in a parent-teacher conference extends and enhances words with nonverbal and nonrecordable nuances that enrich and further elaborate the message.

As a school staff devotes inservice time to the development of sophistication and skill in parent conferencing, increased knowledge and satisfaction of all participants, parents, teachers and students should result.

For additional information:

Improving Parent Conferences. Madeline Hunter and Gerda Lawrence. TIP Publications, P.O. Box 514, El Segundo, California 90245 (in press).

DEVELOPING DISCRIMINATORS, TATTLING OR REPORTING?

MEETING PLAN

This plan is a prototype for any situation when students have trouble discriminating "when to" and "when not to." Additional dilemmas, common to all students, are listed at the end of the meeting plan.

Long Range Objective

Students will report what should be reported and not tattle what should not be tattled.

Staff Meeting Objectives

Teachers will define the difference between tattling and reporting.

Teachers will develop learning opportunities that enable students to discriminate between tattling and reporting.

Teachers will develop strategies to encourage responsible reporting and eliminate tattling. Teachers will role play strategies in staff meeting then use those strategies in their daily interaction with students.

Preparation for Staff Meeting

Before the meeting, teachers should be encouraged to identify in their own words the difference between tattling and reporting and ways that they could make that difference clear to their students so the same discriminator could be applied to any situation the student encountered.

The essential difference between tattling and reporting is a motivational one. A person is tattling when the purpose is to get attention for him/herself and/or to get another person in trouble. (S)he is reporting when the only motive is assistance to someone.

In tattling, the tattletale does nothing to assist the situation but goes directly to the authority figure. When the motive is assistance, the student often will try to do something appropriate to assist the situation before (s)he seeks teacher aid. Only the student knows for sure what his/her motive is, but the teacher can make assumptions and test those assumptions through actions and/or by questioning the student as to his/her purpose.

Unfortunately, the severity of the situation can cloud the discrimination between tattling and reporting. A teacher can erroneously assume that, because (s)he needs to know about it, when a student tells something serious ("Bob and Jim are having a fight") (s)he is reporting. If (s)he reports something mundane ("Tom took an extra piece of paper"), the teacher assumes (s)he is tattling because it is not something important.

It will help to clarify the difference if teachers look at the example of a person calling the police because he sees a stranger climbing in the window of his neighbor's house. Clearly he is reporting. He is trying to assist his neighbor, not get an unknown person in trouble. If, however, the thief's accomplice gets mad at him and "rats" to the police, even though he took the same action as the neighbor, he is tattling.

Teachers rightly feel that they need to know about serious instances of fighting, larceny and other undesirable actions. They must take care, however, that they are not encouraging the tattletales of the school by rewarding "busy body" behavior. Conversely, they need to encourage reporting of important information by children who are confused about "ratting" on a friend.

The complexity of the problem will be appreciated if teachers spend some time identifying the same kinds of decisions they face in their own lives. Should they report the teacher who often misses yard duty? the teacher who is doing unproductive things with students? the teacher who tries to teach without adequate preparation? the principal who doesn't meet responsibilities? the friend who is cheating on his income tax? the person who is saying damaging things about another person? It's easy to discriminate between tattling and reporting for someone else but it's not so easy in our own lives.

Staff Discussion

Teachers must focus on the *motivational* difference between tattling and reporting. To do this, it is helpful if with *each* example they identify those conditions under which an action would be tattling and those conditions when the same action would be reporting. For example, John tells his teacher that Paul took an extra piece of paper. Under what conditions would his statement be reporting and under what conditions would it be tattling?

Reporting—There is only one sheet of paper available for each student. If one student takes two it will mean that someone will not have paper. John has explained this to the culprit and suggested, under the circumstances, he reconsider and return the extra paper. He was unsuccessful so he sought teacher assistance.

Tattling—There is plenty of paper. John didn't check to see if the other student had a valid reason for securing the second piece but came directly to the teacher to report the "sin."

Another example: Mary comes to the teacher to tell that Bob hit Alice. Under what conditions would this action be reporting and under what conditions would it be tattling?

Reporting—Mary, in assessing the situation, has determined that (a) Alice did nothing to deserve being hit (a rare occurrence indeed!), (b) Alice is incapable of protecting herself, (c) Alice is physically hurt, not just offended, (d) Mary can do nothing to make the situation better without teacher intervention.

Tattling—Mary doesn't know (a) whether Alice triggered the attack, (b) whether being hit is part of Alice's "come hither" plan for Bob, (c) it's not a serious situation and will "blow over," (d) Mary's motives are to seek attention from the teacher or she wishes Bob would pay attention to her.

Obviously the examples should be adapted to the real occurrences at school, but once teachers have established that almost any action can be either tattling or reporting, depending on the conditions under which it occurred, they need to develop teaching strategies that will help a student *identify* his motives. Role playing typical situations should be practiced so teachers' questioning become proficient and student responses can be anticipated and productively met. Questions asked the student, such as the following, are helpful:

What have you done to help?

What will happen if we don't do anything?

How serious is it, is anybody really hurt?

Why are you telling me about it?

Have you said anything to the people involved?

Role playing extemporaneous situations in staff meetings is not only laugh promoting, but seeing another teacher's responses suggests possibilities that each staff member can adapt to his/her own style in later interactions with students.

It is also very growth promoting for a staff if a teacher and/or principal demonstrates a discussion with a group of students to enable

125

those students to discriminate between actions which are tattling and those that are reporting. If a videotape is available, this discussion could be held during class time and replayed at a subsequent staff meeting. If videotaping is not possible, there are always students who would be willing to remain after school to be discussants for a staff meeting.

Don't worry if such a demonstration is not perfect, very few demonstrations are. From seeing it in action, teachers are better able to adapt strategies to the needs of students in their own classrooms.

Follow-up

An important outcome of education is the development of discriminators that can be used to clarify situations and suggest appropriate action. This type of inservice meeting which focuses on "factoring out" valid and useful discriminators develops professional skills which can be transferred to other situations where ambiguity may exist. These situations could range from obeying school rules (Under what conditions could you leave the playground without permission?) to the development of precision and artistry with vocabulary. (Under what circumstances would you use the word "confused" and how would those circumstances differ so you should use the word, "bewildered?"—an infinitely more valuable learning than the more typical "Look up the meaning of each word and use it in a sentence").

Most adults have developed intuitive discriminators. Intuition is highly operational but inarticulate knowledge. Unfortunately, intuition, because it isn't articulated, can't be transmitted to another person. The experienced teacher "knows" when to pursue an issue with a student and when to let it drop. The student teacher, lacking the critical discriminators "makes a federal case" out of an unimportant issue and lets something go by that later develops into a serious situation. The habit of attempting to identify the signals that should be used to recognize a situation for what it is, can become a professional fountainhead for continuing staff development.

Questions that might be addressed at subsequent staff meetings are:

1. Under what conditions do you insist that a student remain in during part of lunch time or after school to finish his work? Under what conditions don't you?
2. Under what conditions do you deliver an unwelcome message to a parent about her child? ("Bill is not trying and is getting farther behind.") Under what conditions do you not deliver that information?

3. Under what conditions do you deliver an unwelcome message to a fellow teacher? ("You're not carrying your share of the load.") Under what conditions do you ignore the problem, and under what conditions do you talk to somebody else about it? What conditions determine the person you talk to?
4. Under what conditions do you "cover" curricular material and then move on with your class? Under what conditions must that material be learned by each student before (s)he proceeds?

While staff members may not be able to agree on all the critical discriminators in such situations, the discussion is guaranteed to provoke thoughtful consideration that will generate future deliberation rather than pat "recipes" or unconsidered responses to ambiguous situations which are potentially serious.

Principal's Responsibilities

The principal has the responsibility for modeling as well as encouraging and reinforcing staff behavior which indicates a thoughtful professional approach to a situation. "That was just right, what signaled you to do it?" is one way the principal can stimulate the articulation of discriminators being used by teachers. The principal also has the responsibility for examining and stating the discriminators (s)he uses with an irate parent, judgements about teaching, district policies, as well as his/her own priorities and use of time so that information and some skills can be transmitted to the staff.

Of special importance is the articulation of discriminators used when evaluating teaching so each staff member knows the specific factors on which professional performance is being judged. Subsequent staff meetings should be devoted to a discussion of teachers' professional judgements and behaviors, including those which are described in this book. Those are the critical discriminators of teaching excellence in the classroom.

Dividends

As teachers, in their own classrooms, begin to use these strategies with children to help them identify and articulate discriminators, students will develop the ability to discriminate between tattling and reporting as well as "when to" and "when not to" with other issues they confront. As teachers practice responding to students in a way that reinforces reporting and extinguishes tattling, the staff will develop strategies and professional competence that will transfer to many other educational problems. Most important, teachers will develop the habit of discussing professional issues and problems for the purpose of resolving them rather than ventilating their frustration. This increase in professional competence will result in improved instruction which is the most important dividend realized from the time and energy expended in staff meetings.